Leading Kids
to Books
through
MAGIC

Leading Kids to Books through
MAGIC

Caroline Feller Bauer

Illustrated by

Richard Laurent

American Library Association
Chicago and London 1996

While extensive effort has gone into ensuring the reliability of information appearing in this book, the publisher makes no warranty, express or implied, on the accuracy or reliability of the information, and does not assume and hereby disclaims any liability to any person for any loss or damage caused by errors or omissions in this publication.

Developmental editor: Ellen Lehman, Artefact

Project editor: Joan A. Grygel

Cover design and illustration: Richard Laurent

Text design and composition by Dianne M. Rooney in Bembo using QuarkXpress 3.3 on the Macintosh 7100/66

Printed on 50-pound Glatfelter B-16, a pH-neutral stock, and bound in Arrestox C cloth by Braun-Brumfield, Inc.

The paper used in this publication meets the minimum requirements of American National Standard for Information Sciences—Permanence of Paper for Printed Library Materials, ANSI Z39. 48-1992. ∞

Library of Congress Cataloging-in-Publication Data

Bauer, Caroline Feller.
    Leading kids to books through magic / Caroline Feller
Bauer ; illustrated by Richard Laurent.
        p.   cm. — (Mighty easy motivators)
    Includes bibliographical references.
    ISBN 0-8389-0684-2 (alk. paper)
    1. Children's libraries—Activity programs—United
States. 2. Book talks—United States. 3. Conjuring—
United States. 4. Children's literature—Bibliography.
I. Title. II. Series.
Z718.2.U6B38   1996
027.65'5—dc20   95-53049

Printed in the United States of America.

00   5   4   3   2

For Peter
Thanks for a lifetime
of magical moments

Contents

Contents

Acknowledgments

*T*hanks to my fellow compeers of the International Brotherhood of Magicians #96, El Cajon, California; Society of American Magicians #59, Portland, Oregon; Society of American Magicians #76, Miami Beach, Florida; the Academy of Magical Arts/the Magic Castle Club, Hollywood, California; and to Joyce Basch and Don Brodie who introduced me to the wonders of magic.

Permissions

"Baby Chick," by Aileen Fisher, from *That's Why,* Nelson, 1946. Copyright © Aileen Fisher. Reprinted by permission of the author.

Excerpt from *Binya's Blue Umbrella* by Ruskin Bond. Published by Boyds Mills Press [1995]. Reprinted by permission.

"Dear Tom: A Thanksgiving Fable," by Suzanne Williams, from *Cricket Magazine,* November 1989, 17:3. Text copyright © 1989 by Suzanne Williams. Reprinted by permission of the author.

"Fish Story," by Richard Armour, published in *Light Armour,* McGraw-Hill, 1954. Copyright © 1954 by Richard Armour. Reprinted by permission of John Hawkins & Associates, Inc.

"I Eat My Gumdrops," by Freya Littledale, from *I Was Thinking: Poems,* by Freya Littledale. Greenwillow, 1970. Copyright © 1970 by Freya Littledale. Reprinted by permission of Curtis Brown, Ltd.

"I Sometimes Think about Dollar Bills," by John Ciardi, from *The Reason for the Pelican.* Published by Wordson, Boyds Mills Press [1994]. Reprinted by permission.

"Imagine the Magic," "Two Good Books," and "The Magician's Hands," three poems by J. Patrick Lewis, copyright © 1995 by J. Patrick Lewis. Reprinted by permission of the author.

Imagine the Magic

J. Patrick Lewis

Imagine the magic,
Imagine the fun,
Consider the tricks
You can do with just one
Fantastic idea!
Take any old thing—
A photograph, beads, cards
Some scissors or string.
You be the magician!
Now take it from here—
Change seeds into flowers,
Make coins disappear.
Amaze all your friends
With your magic giraffe!
Or pretend that you're sawing
A rabbit in half!

And there's razzle and dazzle
Of stories and verse
(Keep one in your pocket,
Put two in your purse)
In this little book of magic,
This nifty how-to . . .

Oh, *The Magic of Books*
Is just waiting for you.

The Magic of Magic
A True Story

*H*ere's the sort of experience you could have if you read this book:

Traveling from a small airport in Malaysia, I was asked to open my carry-on case at security. I'm sure the security officers had seen the small pair of scissors I carry.

One of the officers pointed to a bag on the top of my case and asked me, "What's that?" Seizing any opportunity to perform a magic trick, I replied happily, "It's a magic trick. Want to see it?" Before the officers had time to say, "No," or "That's not necessary," I extracted the bag and showed them that it was empty.

"As you see," I said, "there is nothing in this bag. Let me put in these three silk scarves. They are red, blue, and yellow, representing the three primary colors. With the addition of black, I can create any color in the world. In fact, I can show you all the colors of the world as represented by all these flags of the countries of the world—including Malaysia."

I pulled a string of 20 silk flags from the bag and took my bow.

As I finished the trick and started to walk into the waiting room, the telephone on the table rang. One of the security officers picked it up and spoke in his own language. Switching to English he handed me the phone and said, "It's for you."

Astonished, I reached for the phone. A voice said, "I'm the chief of security and I've been observing you from above. Will you show me the trick, too?"

I obliged and though I couldn't see him, performed to a white ceiling. I guess he was up there ... somewhere. As I continued into the waiting room, followed by my bemused husband and a backed up crowd of passengers who had been waiting for their turn at security, I said, "They never did look for the scissors!"

That makes for a pretty good travel story, I think, but it lacks the primary thrust of this book: using magic to introduce literature. Next time I pass through Kerteh, Malaysia, I'll be sure to take with me a book about flags, colors, or worldwide friendship to use in a follow-up booktalk.

Getting Started

I have been playing with magic and books for twenty-five years. I know this because I just received a certificate from the Society of American Magicians for my continued membership for a full quarter century. This year I will earn the same honor from the International Brotherhood of Magicians. I am also a magician member of the Magic Castle, a private club and performing restaurant in Los Angeles, California, for which you must audition in front of a panel of fellow magicians. I tell you this so that you will be duly impressed with my credentials. Although I often use magic in my presentations, I enjoy mostly simple tricks or commercial effects. In other words, with just a little practice, *anyone* can do the tricks I've shared with you here.

I've written this book to introduce you and your children to the magic of reading through magic itself. In my lectures and seminars around the world, I've found that magic can be a powerful way to present literature to both young people and adults. In my experience, even the most sophisticated user of the Internet cannot fail to be intrigued by a dazzling card or coin manipulation. It's been said that there are no new book plots, only writers who bring new perspectives to familiar themes. I think the same can be said for traditional magic tricks. The way in which a trick is performed gives it new life at every showing. By pairing magic and books, you add a special new element to every magic trick you perform.

My audiences of all ages are fascinated by magic. So I urge you to try these tricks (or "effects" as magicians call them) and their accompanying stories and poems with both children and adults, including your students who are learning English as a second language. I've also included examples of literature in French, German, and Spanish that you might enjoy sharing with your second language acquisition students.

As you read, you will find that I've provided simple tricks and directions for performing them, along with ways to introduce literature, including poems to read or recite and stories to tell. I suggest that you tell the story or poem *before* you perform the effect. Most audiences are so thrilled with magic that it's hard to draw their attention back to reading once they've watched a trick performed.

Unless the trick is meant to promote reading in general, I have also provided you with a short book list tailored to the theme of the trick. Display as many of these books as you can, or choose your own favorites to share.

The books that are listed are mostly in the picture book format since they are short and colorful and enjoyed by nearly everyone. If you don't have access to the particular titles listed, don't worry. Simply go to your library catalog and look for other titles on the same subject. I've purposely chosen subjects that are popular in children's literature.

Please Read This!

This is for those of you who, like me, hate to read directions and don't always understand them when you do take the time to read them. If you want to be able to perform magic, however, you absolutely will have to read the directions—unless, of course, your Uncle Ken is a magician and can teach you the tricks in person.

Reading the directions for a trick is rather like reading a recipe. Once you know what it means to *fold* in the egg whites or *clarify* the butter, you can follow the directions and create something edible. Well, anyway, my daughter seems to be able to do it. Don't accept an invitation to a dinner I cook!

Once you've carefully read the directions and practiced the mechanics of an effect, you will want to be certain that you perfect your patter and presentation. *Patter* refers to what the magician says while performing. It is usually not enough to simply follow the directions enclosed with a trick, for it is often what you say that makes a trick amazing. As you become more proficient as a magician, you will find yourself developing your own personal style of patter and presentation.

The general rule to remember is "If Caroline can do it, so can I!"

What to do or say if . . .

Someone asks, *"How did you do that?"*

In Battle Creek, Michigan, a fifth grader came up to me after a magic and literature presentation and said,

"How did you do the trick with the ribbons?" "Sorry," I replied, "I can't tell . . ." Before I could finish he said, "Just checking to see if you're a real magician, because I know a real magician would never tell how she did a trick!"

One reason that performing magic is so satisfying is that your audience is guaranteed never to be bored. But even though children and adults enjoy being fooled, their curiosity often leads them to wonder: "How did she do that?" As a teacher or librarian or parent, you will be delighted that your children are inquisitive and eager to question. As a magician, however, you never want to reveal your secrets (unless, of course, you plan to teach your audience to perform magic tricks). A simple but firm, "I'm sorry, I can't tell you because magicians don't reveal their secrets," should suffice.

Someone blurts out, "I know how you did that!"

The child or adult who knows or thinks she knows how you did the trick wants to show off her knowledge. As before, you can simply say: "Wonderful. Of course you know that magicians never reveal their secrets, so don't tell anyone, even me."

A volunteer is required.

Some of the ideas in this book suggest that the magician (you!) use a volunteer from the audience when one is called for. Many magicians like to involve the audience by asking children or adults to help them on stage. It does take some experience to work well with a perfect stranger, but many of you are classroom teachers, school media specialists, parents, public librarians, and club leaders who know most of the people in your audience. The best advice I can give you about using a volunteer is to keep your sense of humor. If someone says "Yes" instead of "No," simply make a joke out of it. "You said 'Yes?' You're supposed to say 'No.' Whose side are you on, anyway?" Then smile and go on with the show.

The trick doesn't work.

The tricks in this book are fairly foolproof, but if you don't prepare properly or are not paying careful attention, a trick can fail. Since most of these tricks are part of a book program, why not just say, "Whoops. It didn't work. I'll have to practice more and show this to you another day." Then continue with your book presentation. Usually, I don't even announce that I'm going to do a trick. That way, if it doesn't work I can more easily switch gears!

You can't think of a way to relate the effect to a book.

My purpose in writing this book is to encourage you to use magic to introduce literature to children. If your imagination is on hold and you can't think of a way to incorporate reading or books into an effect you wish to present, remember that you can always refer your audience to the many magic books in the library. Reading the directions in a book takes concentration and patience, and your children who take the time to learn how to "read magic" will be happy to perform for you.

My Three Tried-and-True Rules of Magic

Here are three general rules of magic performance that are guaranteed to ensure your success!

Practice, practice, practice the trick before you perform it.

Don't repeat a trick to the same audience on the same day.

Never reveal the secret of a trick, for once told, the magic is gone.

Teaching Tricks to Children

I know I've just emphasized that true magicians never tell how a trick is done. But there's one exception I need to mention: It's perfectly permissible to teach magic to your children.

Yes, learning a magic trick can be "educational." Children learn how to read directions, and they learn the discipline that comes from practicing an art over and over again until it is perfect. Learning magic can also help children gain good hand/eye coordination, develop their imaginations, and hone their skills in logic, writing, and speaking. If you think you might like to teach magic to your children, here are some recommendations:

Make learning a magic trick a reward. Don't indiscriminately show everyone "how to do it."

Be a little greedy with your tricks. Teach only one at a time, and allow some time to elapse before you teach a new trick.

Develop your group's imagination. After your students learn the secret of a trick, let them develop their own patter, based on books or reading.

Keep for yourself the tricks that take extensive preparation. Use of the Change Bag and the Magic Picture are examples of effects better left to you, the "professional." Crayon Color and the Magic of Recycling are good tricks to teach children.

My editor, Ellen Lehman, and I have tried very hard to make the directions for these effects clear, but reading directions takes time and discipline. Have your children read the directions on their own and figure out how the trick is accomplished. Or show your group how to do a trick, and ask the children to show it back to you, then write their own directions.

When your group clamors for "more magic, please," send them to the library shelves to find magic in books.

The Magic Door to Books

The magician walks through a piece of paper.

YOU WILL NEED
construction paper, at least 8 1/2″ × 11″. (Any paper
    or light cardboard will do.)
scissors

Optional: The paper may have the title of the book
you plan to introduce written on it, or you may draw
a door on the paper.

PREPARATION
You'll want to practice this several times before you
try performing it. First, fold the paper in half. At the
fold, make cuts every half inch, from the fold to a half
inch before the edge of the paper. Be careful not to
cut through the edge of the paper. Turn the folded
paper over and cut between the cuts you have already
made, stopping a half inch before the fold. Now snip
each fold except the first and last ones a quarter inch
in from the side. When you pull on the edges, you
will have a giant circle to walk through.

Hint

If you are using ordinary typing paper, be careful
not to tear the circle as you walk through it.

1. FOLD THE PAPER
   IN HALF

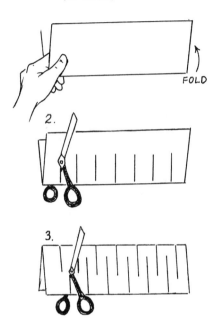

FOLD

2.

3.

CUT ALONG THE
DOTTED LINE SHOWN
HERE — BUT DON'T
CUT THE ENDS!

PATTER AND PRESENTATION

Once you've mastered the effect, try cutting and speaking at the same time. If possible, try to make your patter last as long as the cutting process. Talk about a specific title or about the idea of getting into a good book. Here is what you might say as you cut through the paper:

> I love to read. My family is always complaining that when I read I seem so far away that no one can reach me. It's true! I am far away, deep inside the book. This is what it's like: Pretend that this paper is the book I'm reading. The cover of the book is the door to my imagination. The words are like this pair of scissors. As I read, the story, the characters, and the setting all become part of me. Whether I'm reading an adventure story, a play, a poem, or even the *World Almanac,* I seem to be able to step right into the book, just like I'm doing here. Bye now. See you when I get to the last page!

Choose a Bird

THE EFFECT

A volunteer points to one of five cards, each illustrated with a bird in a different color. The magician shuffles the cards. After eliminating four of the birds with a counting out rhyme, she reveals the chosen bird.

YOU WILL NEED

5 cards, 5″ × 4″, each with a bird drawn in a different color (If you wish, you may duplicate and enlarge the bird drawn on page 16.)

5 envelopes in which to place the birds

4″ 5 CARDS
5″
5 ENVELOPES

Optional: a stand for the envelopes. Ask a handy relative or someone at your local lumber yard to cut a 1/8″ to 1/4″ groove, 1″ deep, along the middle of a 2″ × 2′ board. Or glue 2″

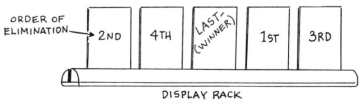

ORDER OF ELIMINATION → | 2ND | 4TH | LAST (WINNER) | 1ST | 3RD |

DISPLAY RACK
2-INCH-HIGH QUARTER ROUNDS

high quarter-rounds to a board as shown in the illustration. This way, you can stand the envelopes up in the slit, leaving your hands free to manipulate the cards. If you have a smaller group you can lay the cards on a table.

PATTER AND PRESENTATION

There are many varieties of birds, but these five cards represent one species: Billy Book Bird. Each bird is a different color: red, yellow, blue, green, and orange.

Display each of the bird cards as you speak.

I also have five bird houses.

Show the five envelopes.

Jennifer (your volunteer), would you please point to the color of your choice? Jennifer has chosen the red bird (or whatever color she has selected).

I'm going to put her bird in its house.

Place in envelope.

All the other birds will go in their houses.

Place each bird in a different envelope.

Now I'll mix up the bird houses.

As you shuffle the envelopes, keep track of which envelope holds the red bird. One way of doing this is to put a tiny mark somewhere on the envelope, making sure that you put the chosen card into that envelope.

Remember that Jennifer has chosen the red bird. The birds are lined up on this telephone pole sleeping in their houses.

Place the five envelopes in a line in your stand, making sure that the chosen card is in the middle.

Now let's cheer for Billy Book Bird. We'll say, "Billy Book Bird, Billy Book Bird, we love you." Each time we chant, I'll eliminate one bird house. But if Jennifer is to win, I can't select the one containing the bird Jennifer has chosen. Let's practice: "Billy Book Bird, Billy Book Bird, we love you."

As each word is said, point to each envelope in turn, starting at one end of the row. When you reach the other end, go back to the beginning again and continue. Remove the envelope indicated on the last word of your rhyme. The trick works automatically! And it doesn't matter which end of the row you start from so long as you start from the same end each time. When three of the cards are eliminated there will be just two left on the stand or table. No need to reveal the final losing card, just discard it and open the last envelope, which contains your volunteer's red bird.

It's red! Jennifer is the winner. Let's give her a big hand.

Hint

You may want to eliminate the "bird houses." If you do, simply face the birds toward you or lay them on the table and with a flourish reveal which bird has been eliminated.

Books to Share

Allen, Judy. *Eagle.* Art by Tudor Humphries. Candlewick, 1994. On a school field trip in the Philippines, Miquel fears a soaring eagle.

Auch, Mary Jane. *Bird Dogs Can't Fly.* Art by author. Holiday, 1993. A dog makes friends with a migrating duck.

Bennett, Penelope. *Town Parrot.* Art by Sue Heap. Candlewick, 1995. Meet a parrot who lives with a person.

Cannon, Janell. *Stellaluna.* Art by author. Morrow, 1993. A baby bat is raised by a family of birds.

Coleman, Evelyn. *The Foot Warmer and the Crow.* Art by Daniel Minter. Macmillan, 1994. A crow advises a slave, and the slave gains his freedom.

Keller, Holly. *Grandfather's Dream.* Art by author. Greenwillow, 1994. A grandfather plans to bring the cranes back to postwar Vietnam.

Torres, Leyla. *Subway Sparrow.* Art by author. Farrar, 1993. In a subway car in New York, a loose sparrow is chased by three people, speaking different languages.

The Change Bag

The change bag is a primary prop for a magician, so I definitely recommend that you invest in one. Any magic supplier anywhere in the world can supply you with one, but you might consider making your own, using the directions below. This way, it will have the advantage of looking less obvious. (Many savvy children will recognize a commercial change bag as a magic prop!)

THE EFFECT

The change bag has two compartments, allowing you to magically "change" one item into another. For instance, you can show the bag empty by turning it inside out. Then place four quarters in the bag and pull out a dollar. Or place pieces of paper, each printed with an individual word, in the bag, then pull out a banner with the words or letters in a sentence. Or put colored silks in the bag and pull out a string of silks or flags.

YOU WILL NEED

2 pieces of fabric, 20″ × 10″ (Traditionally the change bag is made from crushed velvet, but anything that appeals to you will work.)

3 strips of the hook side of Velcro 10″ × 10″

3 strips of the loop side of Velcro 10″ × 10″

sewing machine (Or you can take the project to the alterations person at your local cleaners or to your seamstress friend.)

HOW TO MAKE A CHANGE BAG

TAKE 2 PIECES OF FABRIC —

SEW FABRIC TOGETHER ON 3 SIDES TO CREATE A BAG.

20"

10"

SEW STRIPS OF LOOP VELCRO TO EITHER SIDE OF ONE END OF THE BAG. THEN, SEW STRIPS OF HOOK VELCRO TO EITHER SIDE OF THE OTHER END OF THE BAG.

FOLD THE BAG IN HALF, CLOSING IT WITH THE VELCRO TO FORM A SECOND BAG. WHEN YOU CLOSE THE BAG, THERE WILL BE 2 COMPARTMENTS.

SEW THE LAST 2 STRIPS OF VELCRO TO THE BAG SO THAT THE SECOND COMPARTMENT CLOSES.

THIS IS THE NON-SECRET SIDE, NICE AND NOISY AND DISTRACTING WHEN YOU OPEN IT.

Ways to Use a Change Bag

Remember that you will want to use your change bag for many different effects, so it is especially important that you do not reveal its secret. Here are a few magic tricks that work perfectly with a story or poem to share. You can either use the objects I've suggested or stuffed animals or a picture of the objects.

Chickens

■ Put in an egg. Take out a chicken.

Baby Chick

Aileen Fisher

Peck
   peck
      peck
on the warm brown egg.
OUT comes a neck.
OUT comes a leg.

How
   does
      a chick,
who's not been about,
discover the trick
Of how to get out?

Frogs

■ Put in a tadpole. Take out a frog.

Polliwogs
Maxine W. Kumin

Salamanders, toads and frogs
All begin as polliwogs
Hatching out in swampy bogs.

Polliwogs begin as eggs,
First sprout tails and later, legs.
Eggs are laid by mother frogs

Who begin as polliwogs.

Book to Share
Pfeffer, Wendy. *From Tadpole to Frog.* Art by Holly Keller. HarperCollins, 1994. In this beginning science book, the reader follows a tadpole as it changes into a frog.

Color

■ Put in individual colored ribbons. Take out a rainbow scarf.

━━━━━━━━━━━

I Eat My Gumdrops
Freya Littledale

I eat my gumdrops
one at a time.
Red, yellow, orange, purple—
I have a rainbow
inside of me.

Book to Share

O'Neil, Mary. *Hailstones and Halibut Bones: Adventures in Color.* Art by John Wallner. Doubleday, 1989.

■ Put in a yellow scarf and a blue scarf. Take out a green scarf.

Books to Share

Lionni, Leo. *Little Blue and Little Yellow.* Art by author. Astor-Honor, 1959. Watch as Little Blue and Little Yellow turn into green.

Rossetti, Christina. *Color.* Art by Mary Teichman. Harper, 1992. "What Is Red? What Is Blue?" Rossetti's poem is colorfully illustrated.

■ Put in a red scarf, a white scarf, and a blue scarf. Take out a flag of the United States.

Book to Share
Wallner, Alexandra. *Betsy Ross.* Art by author.
Holiday, 1994. Follows the design and sewing of
the first American flag.

(Other nations with flags of red, white, and blue
are France, Iceland, Dominican Republic, Cuba, Tai-
wan, Chile, Liberia, Norway, New Zealand, Paraguay,
Thailand.)

Money

■ Put in coins. Take out bills.

I Sometimes Think about Dollar Bills
John Ciardi

I sometimes think when I'm alone
It would be very strange
Should I become a dollar bill
And meet myself in change.

I think it would be rather hard—
Considering the times—
To leave myself in pennies
And meet myself in dimes.

The hardest part of it would be—
As you well realize—
That when I met myself, I'd be
Hard to recognize.

Books to Share

Brisson, Pat. *Bennie's Pennies.* Art by Bob Barner. Doubleday, 1993. What can Bennie buy with five pennies for his family?

Maestro, Betsy. *The Story of Money.* Art by Giulio Maestro. Clarion, 1993. Surveys the history of money and shows how money is printed.

Parker, Nancy Winslow. *Money, Money, Money: The Meaning of the Art and Symbols on United States Paper Currency.* Art by author. Harper, 1995. Explore the history of our paper currency.

Schwartz, David M. *How Much Is a Million?* Art by Steven Kellogg. Lothrop, 1985. A splendid survey of all matters money. See also Schwartz's *If You Made a Million.* Lothrop, 1989.

Butterflies

■ Put in a caterpillar. Take out a butterfly.

Books to Share

Carle, Eric. *The Very Hungry Caterpillar.* Art by author. Philomel, 1969. The classic story of a caterpillar who eats all week long and finally turns into a beautiful butterfly.

Hariton, Anca. *Butterfly Story.* Art by author. Dutton, 1995. The life cycle of a butterfly with art to share.

Photography

■ Put in a blank card. Take out a photograph.

Books to Share

Castle, Caroline, and Peter Bowman. *Grandpa Baxter and the Photographs.* Art by Peter Bowman. Orchard, 1993. Grandpa Baxter Bear and his grandson spend the day looking at the family photos.

McPhail, David. *Pig Pig and the Magic Photo Album.* Art by author. Dutton, 1986. Say "cheese" and Pig Pig ends up in a variety of places while taking a photo.

Music

■ Put in music notes. Take out a cassette player that is playing music or a musical instrument (such as a harmonica or recorder) to play.

Books to Share

Martin, Bill, Jr. *The Maestro Plays.* Art by Vladimir Radunsky. Holt, 1994. Bright bold art accompanies the maestro while he plays.

Moss, Lloyd. *Zin! Zin! Zin! a Violin*. Art by Margorie Priceman. Simon and Schuster, 1995. Play along with this rhythmic romp.

Steig, William. *Zeke Pippin*. Art by author. Harper, 1994. Zeke foils a gang of thieves when he plays his harmonica.

More Ideas for Your Change Bag

Put in beads. Take out a necklace.

Put in seeds. Take out a flower or fruit.

Put in words. Take out a banner, book title, or book.

Coloring Book

You can purchase a magic coloring book from many magic dealers or make your own.

THE EFFECT
Show the black-and-white pages of a coloring book. Say a few magic words and show that the pages have been colored.

YOU WILL NEED
coloring book	scissors
crayons	patience!

PREPARATION
Beginning on the first page of the coloring book, cut a strip a quarter of an inch from the top right-hand corner down the side of the book to the center. Do this on every other page. On the second page (and every other page after) cut a strip a quarter of an inch wide from the bottom up.

By flipping the pages at the top half of the book, you will see only every other page in the book. By flipping the bottom half, you will see only the other pages.

Color every other page in the book. This is when you'll need patience, for you may find that you don't enjoy coloring as much as you did when you were six. Be careful not to color the wrong pages! You don't want to start all over again.

CUT THE FIRST PAGE LIKE THIS.

CUT THE SECOND PAGE LIKE THIS.

If you buy a commercial magic coloring book from a magic dealer, you will probably purchase a three-way book that allows you to show blank pages, black-and-white outline drawings, and the same drawings in color. You can talk about writing or illustrating using the commercial book and show the blank pages that a writer or illustrator begins with.

Optional: Cover the coloring book with a book jacket, disguising the purchased coloring book.

PATTER AND PRESENTATION
Begin by teaching your students a magic phrase. One of my favorites is: Color Craze! Let them practice a few times. Then begin:

When you admire the art in a picture book you might wonder how the artist draws the pictures. I happen to have the preliminary drawings for this book. The artist first sketched outlines of the pictures she wanted to make,

Show the black-and-white drawings in the coloring book.

Later, when she had time, she said a few magic words: Color Craze!

Ask the children to say them with you.

And the pictures are magically colored!

Show the colored pictures.

Suggestion: If you want your audience to help you "color" the illustrations, show the black-and-white outline side of the book. Ask the children to look at what they are wearing. Those who are wearing red can toss some red into the book. Those wearing blue can add blue, and so on. You can clown around, saying, as you reach up or around for a color thrown, "Aim for the book. We don't want the colors to land all over the place!" Then show the colored pictures they have helped to color!

Magic dealers will have other suggestions for "magically" painting the coloring book, such as paint palettes and magical crayons.

Books to Share
Share books featuring color. (See Books to Share on pages 21, 83, and 86.)

The Stamp Album

THE EFFECT
An empty stamp album magically fills with stamps.

YOU WILL NEED
empty stamp album from a stamp or hobby shop
used stamps collected from envelopes or a packet of
     foreign stamps purchased from
     a stamp or hobby shop
glue
scissors

PREPARATION
Prepare the stamp
album as you did
the coloring book.
Cut every other
page either from
the top or from the
bottom so that alter-
nating pages will show
every other page when
you flip through the book.

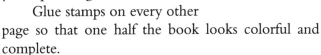

    Glue stamps on every other
page so that one half the book looks colorful and
complete.

PATTER AND PRESENTATION
I'd like to read you a poem.

Stamps

Siv Widerberg

> I collected stamps
> Papa gave me a big bagful
> I didn't collect stamps anymore.

It's true. I used to collect stamps, but now I don't. The reason? I'm too lazy to sort through the stamps, find the correct country, and paste the stamps into the book in the proper place. This is what the album looks like without stamps.

Flip the book showing only the black-and-white outlines.

Lucky for me I know a little magic. By reciting just a few words of magic (say magic words of your choice), I can magically paste the postage stamps into the album.

Flip the side that shows the stamps.

Share another poem about stamps or display the books listed under Books to Share.

———

Stamps
Linda G. Paulsen

You can lick 'em
    and stick 'em
And send them away;
Or keep 'em on hinges
    In an album's OK.

You can trade 'em
    parade 'em,
Or save 'em forever;
Compare 'em and share 'em
    most any endeavor.

You can buy 'em
    or sell 'em,
From most anywhere;
Collect every color
    and size to compare.

You can display 'em,
    or lay 'em
Under a lamp.
What are they? I'll tell you:
The postage stamp.

Books to Share
Ahlberg, Janet, and Allan Ahlberg. *The Jolly Postman.*
    Art by Allan Ahlberg. Little, 1986. Removable
    letters to and from folktale characters.

Granger, Neill. *Stamp Collecting.* Illustrated. Millbrook, 1994. Everything you've wanted to know about stamp collecting and even a little more.

Grossman, Samuel. *Stamp Collecting Explained* Running Press, 1988. A good introduction to stamp collecting.

Lewis, Brenda R. *Stamps! A Young Collector's Guide.* Dutton, 1991. A picture-book–sized overview of stamp collecting.

Share any book about another city, state, or country that you would like to visit, or discuss stamp collecting as a hobby.

Card Tricks

The favorite activity for a rainy day when I was growing up in various cities of the United States was playing cards. We continued to play intense games of War even after we had graduated to real card games. When I was sixteen I spent the summer with a French family on a horse farm near the city of Nancy. We spent the whole summer in the garden, in the salon, in the dining room, and even in the stable playing Canasta. I was in love with all three of the older boys in the family, but I was in awe of Michel, who impressed us with his magical dexterity with a repertoire of card tricks.

Do children still play Solitaire when they are home alone? Do they play Hearts with their friends? I have a feeling that television and videos have taken the place of a good card game. What a shame. Cards are so portable and the games are international.

Even before the invention of printing it appears that people were playing cards. In 1392 Charles VI of France commissioned a painter to illuminate three decks of cards. The painter designed the four suits of hearts, diamonds, spades, and clubs; the court cards; and the colors of red and black. Originally the deck represented life in the Middle Ages. Although there are many variations on this original theme, the cards we use today are very similar to those invented more than 600 years ago. Bring back cards to your community! Teach some age-appropriate games to your group, and introduce them with a few simple tricks.

The Accordion Shuffle

This is a sight gag that makes a perfect introduction to shuffling the cards for a trick or game.

THE EFFECT
You appear to be a master card shark when you take a pack of cards and manipulate it by tossing the cards from one hand to the other.

YOU WILL NEED
deck of playing cards

staple gun

PREPARATION
Staple each card to the next card on opposite sides so that when they are held up they will be fastened accordion style. No need to use the whole deck of cards! Use a deck that is missing a few cards. An older deck will be more flexible, too.

PATTER AND PRESENTATION

You have probably seen card players in the movies or on television who expertly shuffle the cards. Anyone can do it. All you need is a deck of cards and a lot of nerve.

Hold the cards in your right hand cupped over your left hand. Pull them up and down once or twice. You want to show that the maneuver is a joke before the audience catches on. Now pull the cards out sideways so that the audience sees that they are stapled together.

Blank Card Shuffle

Here's another good introduction to a card game or a trick.

YOU WILL NEED
deck of playing cards

blank face card (Make a blank face card by trimming a white index card to fit the spare joker in a deck of cards. Glue it to the face of the card.)

PREPARATION
Put the blank card on the top of the deck. The pips, or numbers on the cards, are only on the left side of the cards. When you fan the cards to the left, counterclockwise, the corners of the cards will be empty and the deck will look blank. You may need to practice this quite a bit to avoid showing the audience the pictures on the cards. When you fan the cards to the right, clockwise, the audience will see the card numbers.

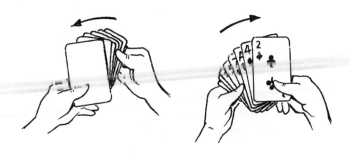

PATTER AND PRESENTATION

Cards have been around for a long time. People were playing cards at least 600 years ago. It's a good thing that the printing press was invented or we would have to paint the numbers and suits on each card or play with blank cards. Maybe that would be a good idea. I could always say that I have a winning hand!

I was astonished when I opened this new deck of cards. They are all blank.

Fan the cards to the left, but take care not to go past the blank corners. Square the cards.

I guess it wouldn't be very fair to play with a deck of blank cards. It wouldn't even be much fun. How could you tell if you were winning or losing? I'll just say a few magic words: "Card Shark!" and turn these blank cards into a deck of ordinary cards.

Remove the blank card from the top of the deck and place it on the bottom of the deck. Fan the cards to the right, revealing the numbers.

Forcing a Card

Many card tricks reveal a card chosen by a member of the audience. There are several ways to "force" the volunteer to choose a card. This method is simple and easy to perform.

YOU WILL NEED
deck of playing cards
table
volunteer

PATTER AND PRESENTATION
Pick up a pack of cards and fan it toward you so that you see what number and suit are on the bottom of the deck. Square the cards and place the pack on the table.

> May I have a volunteer to cut the cards by taking part of the pack and placing it on the table?

Pick up the bottom half of the deck and place it on the top half. Your force card is now on the top of the bottom half. When you place the top pack of cards on the bottom pack, place it so that it is slightly askew. Pick up the top half again, leaving the force card on top of the bottom half.

> Would you (volunteer) please take the top card from the top of the bottom half?

Announce what it is, and let the volunteer prove you right!

Predicting the Future

THE EFFECT
You predict what card will appear on the top of the deck.

YOU WILL NEED
deck of cards and some chutzpah (Yiddish for a lot of nerve!)

PREPARATION
Practice holding the cards in front of you with the backs of the cards toward a mirror (the audience). Glance at the card facing you and remember it. Put the deck behind your back and switch the bottom card to the top of the deck. Hold the deck in front of you. Predict the number and suit of the card facing the audience and show that you are right.

While the cards are in front of you, note the card facing you, your next prediction. Repeat the process of putting the cards behind you and switching the bottom card to the top of the deck. Don't look guilty! You are a magician, confident of your astounding abilities.

PATTER AND PRESENTATION
I've brought a pack of cards with me today to show you that I have learned to predict the future. Would someone volunteer to shuffle the cards?

Cards are shuffled and returned to you.

Now I will put the cards behind my back and gaze into the future. I see a red card—no, maybe it's black. Of course, it's red. It's the three of hearts. (Or whatever card you've chosen.)

Make sure to be a little corny about the predicted card. You can repeat this trick two or three times, but more savvy children may catch on if you repeat it too often.

And now that I have shown you that I can predict the future, I predict that I will read to you—.

Choose a favorite book to read or share Lloyd Alexander's *The Fortune Tellers*.

Books to Share

BOOKS FEATURING CARD GAME RULES

Cole, Johanna, and Stephanie Calmenson. *Crazy Eights and Other Card Games*. Art by Alan Tiegreen. Morrow, 1994. In addition to the rules for 20 games, this book describes a deck of cards and how to deal.

Gem Card Games: An Expert Guide to More Than 100 Card Games. Running Press, 1994. The games are divided into two sections: Family Games and Children's Games. They include clear, simple directions in a small, portable format.

Sheinwold, Alfred. *101 Family Card Games*. Art by Myron Miller. Sterling, 1992. How to deal, how to play, and how to win.

BOOKS FEATURING CARD TRICKS

For Children

Bailey, Vanessa. *Rainy Day Card Tricks.* Watts, 1990. Color photos demonstrate simple card sleights and handling for basic card tricks.

For Adults

Longe, Bob. *World's Best Card Tricks.* Sterling, 1992. Card tricks are arranged by method.

Wilson, Mark. *Mark Wilson's Greatest Card Tricks.* Running Press, 1993. Master the Glide, Double Lift, and the Hindu Shuffle.

GENERAL RESOURCE

U.S. Playing Card Co., 4590 Beech St., Cincinnati, OH 45212. A good source for books, playing cards, and a special teacher packet.

Choose an Author

THE EFFECT
Members of the audience call out the names of favorite authors. The magician writes the names on pieces of paper and places them in a box. A volunteer chooses a piece of paper from the box. The magician correctly guesses the name of the author the volunteer has chosen.

YOU WILL NEED
small pad of paper

pen

empty box, such as a shoe box

PATTER AND PRESENTATION
Everyone here probably has a favorite author. Perhaps you have even read more than one book by this author. Maybe you often recommend the author's books to your friends. If you have a favorite author, please raise your hand. (Point to someone in the audience who has raised her hand.) Who is your favorite author? (Repeat the name of the author as you write the name on a slip of paper.) Who else has a favorite author?

As each person calls out a choice, write a name on another piece of paper. However, do not write the name called out, but instead write the name first called out, so that all the pieces of paper contain the same name. After you write each name, fold the piece of paper and throw it into the box. When you have six or eight names, ask a volunteer to choose a folded piece of paper from the box.

I am thinking of the author whose name is on the piece of paper in your hand. I think I know the name.

As you concentrate on the name on the chosen paper, pick up the remaining papers and crumple them in your hand in order to get rid of the evidence! If you know titles by the author chosen you might repeat a few, showing that you're getting close.

Yes, I do know it! It's . . . (reveal the name of the author chosen). Let's give our volunteer a round of applause and remember the author (author's name). We have his [or her] books in the library.

Hint

Make sure that you look as though you are writing the names called. A long name might take a moment longer to write! You might even ask for the spelling of a name.

Two Good Books
J. Patrick Lewis

If you were a book,
What book would you be?
A Field Guide to Butterflies?
Life in the Sea?

> If I were a book,
> I'd be *Rumplestiltskin,*
> *'Twas the Night Before Christmas,*
> Or *Huckleberry Finn.*

If we were two blockbuster
Books on the shelves,
We'd tingle our spines
Reading us to ourselves . . .

> then we'd do the same thing
> All the other books did—
> We'd wait to be borrowed
> By some lucky kid.

Fractions

A dollar bill changes into four quarters.

YOU WILL NEED

dollar bill	scissors
four quarters	pen or pencil
four envelopes	small table

PREPARATION

Cut the flap off one envelope. Put four quarters into a second envelope and place it, with the flap open, behind the flapless envelope. Place two more envelopes (flaps open) behind the envelope containing the quarters. The extra envelopes will mask the envelope with the quarters.

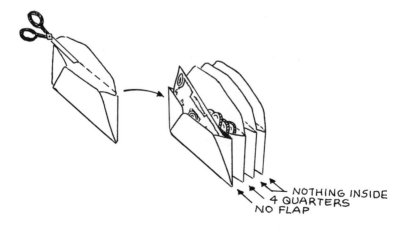

NOTHING INSIDE
4 QUARTERS
NO FLAP

PATTER AND PRESENTATION

> As you know, of course, a dollar can take many forms. Does anyone have a dollar bill?

Take one of the proffered bills. You may wish to plant a dollar bill with one of your audience members in advance.

> Thank you for trusting me. I'm going to use this envelope as a wallet. I'll place your dollar bill in the envelope.

Place the dollar bill into the flapless envelope.

> Please write your first name on this flap.

Put the envelopes onto a table, making sure that the dollar peeks out of the flapless envelope, hiding the fact that the envelope is not a whole one. Let your volunteer write her name on the flap. Pick up the pack of envelopes, lick the envelope with the exposed signed flap and the quarters, and close it. In doing so, steal away the flapless envelope and the remaining envelopes. You might place them face down on the table so that your volunteer doesn't see the envelope with the dollar bill.

> Your dollar is in this envelope. Of course I think that it would be fair if you gave me half of your dollar for giving you the opportunity to be on stage. Think of the story you can tell your family tonight! I'll just cut the dollar in half and we'll share it.

Cut the envelope in half, and pour four quarters onto the table.

Look! Your dollar has turned into four quarters. If you were really nice, you would share your dollar with me. Anyway, I'll share a book with you!

Books to Share

Burns, Marilyn. *The Greedy Triangle*. Art by Gordon Silveria. Scholastic, 1995. A story featuring a hungry triangle and other shapes.

Jonas, Ann. *Splash!* Art by author. Greenwillow, 1995. Add and subtract the animals in a pond.

Leedy, Loreen. *Fraction Action*. Art by author. Holiday, 1994. Miss Prime teaches her animal students about fractions.

Pinczes, Elinor J. *A Remainder of One*. Art by Bonnie Mackain. Houghton, 1995. Ants demonstrate the concept of remainders.

Sandburg, Carl. *Arithmetic*. Art by Ted Rand. Harcourt, 1994. Sandburg's classic poem about math.

Van Der Meer, Ron, and Bob Gardner. *The Math Kit*. Scribner, 1994. This interactive kit explores the world of mathematics.

Dear Tom

This trick is especially appropriate for Thanksgiving, but the story can be used for any holiday involving food—in other words, for almost any holiday!

THE EFFECT
The magician shows an empty envelope. She places a picture of a turkey into the envelope. When she opens the envelope, the turkey has changed into a picture of a cooked turkey lying on a platter.

YOU WILL NEED
picture of Tom Turkey
picture of a cooked turkey
2 envelopes of the same size
glue

PREPARATION
Glue the fronts of two envelopes together so that they appear to be a single envelope. Duplicate the two pictures shown here or draw your own. You may read the story of Tom Turkey from this book, or you can reproduce the letters and place them into a second set of envelopes: the invitations in one, Tom's response in another. As you tell the story, open the appropriate envelope and read.

**PATTER AND
PRESENTATION**

Dear Tom: A Thanksgiving Fable

Suzanne Williams

Tom lived alone at the edge of the woods. He was a quiet sort of creature. He was also a slow thinker.

The other forest animals ignored Tom for the most part. They went about their business while Tom went about his. If Tom chanced to meet one of them, he would waggle his head in greeting and go on his way.

There were times when Tom wished for company, but he was too shy to ask for it. He knew he was not a good-looking fellow. In fact, he was rather awkward-looking. He found comfort in his daily routines: eating, sleeping, gathering seeds and berries, walking, and reading the mail. He never received any letters, of course, but he enjoyed looking at the seed catalogs that came.

So you can imagine Tom's surprise when one cold, crisp November day he opened his mailbox and found three letters. Tom hurried back to his house and put on his reading glasses.

The first letter was an invitation from Fred and Fanny Fox.

"Dear Tom," it said. "Would you be our guest of honor on Thanksgiving Day? We would be delighted to have you."

For goodness sakes, thought Tom. That's certainly nice of them. It's been months since we've passed on the forest path. I wonder what made them think of me now?

He smiled to himself as he put the first invitation aside and picked up the second letter. This one was an invitation from Dr. Benjamin Bobcat.

"My dear Tom," he read. "It would be my pleasure if you would consent to visit my home at 9:00 AM on Thanksgiving Day. My cook has promised a fine dinner."

Well now, thought Tom, isn't that nice. Seems like 9:00 AM is a bit early for a Thanksgiving dinner though. I wonder why he wants me there so early?

The last letter was from the Henry Hawk family. It was addressed to "Tom and His Mrs. and Family." Tom chuckled. "I guess they don't know I'm a bachelor," he said.

"Greetings!" read this third invitation. "The family and I are most anxious to

have you for dinner on Thanksgiving Day.
Please bring your wife and children, too."

When Tom finished reading the last invitation, he took off his glasses and leaned back in his chair, basking in the warmth of his sudden popularity.

"It does a body good to know he's got so many thoughtful friends," he said. He sighed happily and pictured himself dressed in his best suit, tail feathers spread out behind in a handsome fan. Visiting would be fun. He thought about the lonely Thanksgiving feasts he'd had in the past. The food was good: grasshopper casserole, pine nuts, and blackberry cobbler for dessert. But he'd always wished there had been someone to share the meal. He wondered what other folk ate for Thanksgiving dinner.

It was an hour or more before the problem of choosing among the three invitations sank in.

Dear me, worried poor Tom. What shall I do? If I accept just one invitation, the others may feel hurt. I can't possibly be in three places at once!

He brooded and stewed and paced up and down until finally he made up his mind about what to do.

He sat down at his desk, took out paper and pen, and wrote the same reply to each invitation.

I deeply regret that I am unable to accept your kind invitation for dinner. I thank you for the offer and I hope you enjoy your meal.

Yours truly,
Thomas T. Turkey

When Thanksgiving Day arrived, Tom fixed himself a wonderful meal of roasted chestnuts and acorn pancakes with strawberry jam. It was a delicious dinner, and though he ate it alone, he was not lonely. For he had saved the three invitations and he found great pleasure in reading them again and again.

It is better to eat alone than to be eaten.

After telling the story, show the prepared envelope displaying it empty.

Tom went into his house to enjoy his dinner alone.

Place the turkey picture in the envelope.

It's a good thing that he didn't accept any of the invitations or he might have ended up like this.

Turn the envelope around and reach into the second envelope and pull out the picture of the cooked turkey.

Remember that you can easily use this trick for other "before and after" effects. For instance, show a baby and then the woman she becomes, illustrating coming-of-age stories. Drop clothes into the envelope, then pull out someone fully dressed, illustrating stories about fashion. Put seeds into the envelope and pull out a picture of a plant, illustrating books about growing food or gardening.

Fresh Fish Sold Here

The patter for this effect is based on a joke that is told in Eastern Europe, the Middle East, and Latin America. The trick was developed by Arnold Furst, a magician who lives in Los Angeles, California. Make your own version, using the illustration shown here as a guide, or purchase the already printed and prepared banners from a magic supplier.

THE EFFECT
A banner proclaiming FRESH FISH SOLD HERE is displayed to the audience. As a story is told, each word is subsequently torn from the sign. At the end of the story the banner is restored intact.

YOU WILL NEED
2 paper banners with the words FRESH FISH SOLD
   HERE lettered on each

glue

PREPARATION

Fold one of the banners into thirds and then fold in half. Fold it in thirds again, creating a bundle. Glue the folded banner in back of the word FRESH on the second banner. As you tell the story tear off each word as indicated below, folding the torn sheets into your left hand. When you reach the end of the story, unfold the first banner to show that it has been put back together again.

Hint

Naturally you will want to be able to show this trick again, so save the intact banner to glue onto the next banner.

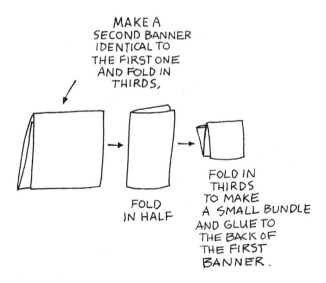

MAKE A
SECOND BANNER
IDENTICAL TO
THE FIRST ONE
AND FOLD IN
THIRDS,

FOLD
IN HALF

FOLD IN
THIRDS
TO MAKE
A SMALL BUNDLE
AND GLUE TO
THE BACK OF
THE FIRST
BANNER.

PATTER AND PRESENTATION

The grand opening of Gustavo's fish shop was an exciting event. He had commissioned a large sign to hang in front of his shop. It said

"FRESH FISH SOLD HERE."

When his son saw the sign, he laughed. "Why did you put the word *here* on the sign? You don't need it. Everyone knows that you're selling the fish here, not across the street! Take out the word *here*."

Gustavo climbed up on a ladder and took down the word *here*.

Tear off the word *here*.

His wife came out and looked at the sign. "Why do you have the word *sold* on the sign? Everyone knows that you are selling fish, not giving it away."

Gustavo climbed up on the ladder and took down the word *sold*.

Tear off the word *sold*.

Gustavo's mother-in-law came outside to admire the sign. "Why do you have the word *fish* on the sign? Anyone can smell the fish when they pass the shop. You don't need the word *fish*."

Gustavo climbed up on the ladder and took down the word *fish*.

Tear off the word *fish*.

Gustavo's daughter stood on the sidewalk and stared at her father's sign. "Why do you have the word *fresh* on the sign?" Obviously your fish is fresh. You wouldn't sell old fish!"

Gustavo climbed up on the ladder and removed the word *fresh*.

Tear off the word *fresh*.

The next day Gustavo's father came to visit the shop. "Where is the sign that I paid for?" he asked.

Gustavo climbed up on the ladder and put back the sign that said "FRESH FISH SOLD HERE."

Fold the pieces you have torn off and unfold the new banner that says

FRESH FISH SOLD HERE.

———

This story would be splendid to tell children and adults who are learning English. It would work equally well with English speakers learning a foreign language. Following is the same story in Spanish.

Aqui Se Vende Pescado Fresco

Translated into Spanish by José Danchin

La gran apertura de la pescadería de Gustavo fue un evento muy emocionante.

El hizo que se colgara oficialmente un letrero grande delante la pescadería, en que decía:

"AQUÍ SE VENDE PESCADO FRESCO."

Cuando su hijo lo vió, se rió de él. ¿Por qué pusiste la palabra *aquí* en el letrero? No es necesario. Todos saben que tú vendes pescado aquí, y no al cruzar la calle. Quita la palabra *aquí*.

Gustavo se subió en una escalera y quitó la palabra *aquí*.

Luego su esposa vino y miró el letrero.

¿Por qué tienes las palabras *se vende* en el letrero? Todos saben que tú los estas vendiendo y no regalando.

Gustavo se subió otra vez en la escalera y quitó las palabras *se vende*.

Despues la hija de Gustavo se paró en la vereda y se fijó en el anuncio de su padre.

¿Por qué tienes la palabra *fresco* en el letrero? Es obvio que tú pescado sea fresco, porque no venderías pescado viejo.

Gustavo se subió nuevamente en la escalera y quitó la palabra *fresco*.

La suegra de Gustavo también salió afuera para admirar el letrero. ¿Por qué tienes la palabra *pescado?* Cualquiera puede oler el olor de pescado cuando pasan por la pescaderia. Tú no necesitas la palabra *pescado.* Gustavo se subió en la escalera y quitó la palabra *pescado.* Al próximo día, el padre de Gustavo vino a visitar la pescadería y le preguntó. ¿Donde está el letrero que pagué por el? Entonces, Gustavo se subió en la escalera y puso el letrero que decía:

AQUÍ SE VENDE PESCADO FRESCO.

Books to Share

Day, David. *The Walking Catfish.* Art by Mark Entwisle. Macmillan, 1992. A three-day liar's contest features a BIG fish.

Coffelt, Nancy. *Tom's Fish.* Art by author. Harcourt, 1994. Tom's goldfish is a special individual.

McKissack, Patricia C. *A Million Fish . . . More or Less.* Art by Dena Schutzer. Knopf, 1992. Hugh Thomas catches a million fish, more or less, in this spirited tall tale.

Wilcox, Cathy. *Enzo the Wonderfish.* Art by author. Ticknor & Fields, 1994. It's not easy to teach a fish to do tricks.

Wu, Norbert. *Fish Faces.* Photos by author. Holt, 1993. Short text accompanies color photographs of fish.

Orange to Apple

An orange becomes an apple.

YOU WILL NEED
orange
apple, smaller than the
    orange
knife
cloth napkin

PREPARATION
Cut the orange in quarters vertically without cutting all the way through at the top. Then, peel away the fruit, leaving the skin. Place the orange peel around the apple with the connected end on top.

PATTER AND PRESENTATION
> I can never decide which I'd rather eat, an apple or an orange. Luckily it doesn't matter, I just eat the orange.

Place the napkin over the orange and remove the peel. When you take away the napkin and peel, you will reveal the apple.

> And I have an apple.

Books to Share

Creasy, Rosalind. *Blue Potatoes, Orange Tomatoes.* Art by Ruth Heller. Sierra Club, 1994. How to grow a garden of rainbow fruit and vegetables.

Lember, Barbara Hirsch. *A Book of Fruit.* Photos by author. Ticknor & Fields, 1994. Hand-tinted photos show fruit up close and growing in the fields and orchards.

Priceman, Marjorie. *How to Make an Apple Pie and See the World.* Art by author. Knopf, 1994. A unique look at the many countries whose products contribute to making an apple pie.

Rogow, Zack. *Oranges.* Art by Mary Szilagyi. Orchard, 1988. The many people from many countries who help to grow and ship oranges.

The Umbrella

Here's an example of a common object that easily becomes a magic surprise.

THE EFFECT
On the last line of a poem about rain or umbrellas, an umbrella opens.

YOU WILL NEED
collapsible umbrella that opens with a touch of a
    button

PATTER AND PRESENTATION
Recite one of these poems. On the last line, open the umbrella and take your bow.

It's Pouring Rain

Charlotte Pomerantz

It's pouring rain,
    hooray hooray.
I can't go out
    to run or play.
So everybody
    go away.
We're going to read
    my books all day.

Here is the same poem in French.

Il Pleut des Cordes

translated by Jane Riles

Il pleut des cordes.
　　Chic, alors!
Je ne peux pas sortir,
　　ni courir, ni jouer.
Donc, tout le monde
　　Allez! Partez!
On va lire mes livres
　　Toute la journée!

Umbrellas
Maxine Kumin

It's raining in the city.
I hope it rains for hours.
All of the umbrellas
Open up like flowers.

Come look out my window!
Polka dots in lines
Wag their stems and tangle,
Tilt to read the signs.

Plaid ones cross at corners,
Striped ones wave about.
It's raining in the city;
The flowers have come out.

Hint

If you recite this on a rainy day, ask your audience
to put up their umbrellas on the last line, too.

Here's a favorite chapter from a rainy day story.

Binya's Blue Umbrella
Ruskin Bond

Most of the people in the village were a little
envious of Binya's blue umbrella. No one else
had ever possessed one like it. The schoolmas-
ter's wife thought it was quite wrong for a poor

farmer's daughter to have such a fine umbrella while she, a second-class college graduate, had to make do with an ordinary black one. When her husband offered to have their old umbrella dyed blue, she gave him a scornful look and loved him a little less than before. The village priest, who looked after the temple, announced that he would buy a multicolored umbrella the next time he was in town. A few days later he returned, looking annoyed and grumbling that they weren't available except in Delhi. Most people consoled themselves by saying that Binya's pretty umbrella wouldn't keep out the rain if it rained heavily, that it would shrivel in the sun if the sun was fierce, that it would collapse in the wind if the wind was strong, that it would attract lightning if lightning fell near it, and that it would prove unlucky if there was any ill luck going about. Secretly, everyone admired it.

Unlike the adults, the children didn't have to pretend. They were full of praise for the umbrella. It was so light, so pretty, so bright a blue! And it was just the right size for Binya. They knew that if they said nice things about the umbrella, Binya would smile and give it to them to hold for a little while—just a very little while!

Soon it was the time of the monsoon. Big black clouds kept piling up, and thunder rolled over the hills.

Binya sat on the hillside all afternoon, waiting for the rain. As soon as the first big drop of rain came down, she raised the umbrella over her head. More drops, big ones, came pattering down. She could see them through the umbrella silk as they broke against the cloth.

And then there was a cloudburst, and it was like standing under a waterfall. The umbrella wasn't really a rain umbrella, but it held up bravely. Only Binya's feet got wet. Rods of rain fell around her in a curtain of slivered glass.

Everywhere on the hillside people were scurrying for shelter. Some made for a charcoal-burner's hut; others for a mule shed, or Ram Bharosa's shop. Binya was the only one who didn't run. This was what she'd been waiting for—rain on her umbrella—and she wasn't in a hurry to go home. She didn't mind getting her feet wet. The cows didn't mind getting wet either.

Presently she found Bijju sheltering in a cave. He would have enjoyed getting wet, but he had school books with him and couldn't afford to let them get spoiled. When he saw Binya, he came out of the cave and shared the umbrella. He was a head taller than his sister, so he had to hold the umbrella for her while she held his books.

The cows had been left far behind.

"Neelu, Neelu!" called Binya.

"Gori!" called Bijju.

When their mother saw them sauntering home through the driving rain, she called out, "Binya! Bijju! Hurry up, and bring the cows in! What are you doing there in the rain?"

"Just testing the umbrella," said Bijju.

The Magic of Recycling

Here's a magic trick that is perfect to use when you are trying to encourage children to be tidy recyclers.

THE EFFECT
A wad of paper flies and lands at your bidding.

YOU WILL NEED
trousers or a pair of jeans (This trick uses the "dead" space in your front pants pocket. Therefore, you need to be wearing trousers or a pair of jeans when performing this "throw-away" effect.)

2 pieces of paper approximately 3″ × 3″

PREPARATION
Before your audience arrives, crush one of the paper squares into a wad of trash. Place it out of sight, under a chair or in a corner.

PATTER AND PRESENTATION
I've noticed that some of you have

become careless about properly disposing your trash. If everyone were to leave their discarded paper scattered all over the room we wouldn't be able to enter this room after just a single day! Don't tell me that the trash accumulates by magic. If you aren't near a wastebasket or a recycling bin, put the trash in your pockets and empty them when you can. Look at my pockets.

Turn your two front pockets out.

They were full of bits of paper just a few minutes ago. Where does the trash go? Even this little piece of paper can add to the trash problem.

Show your audience the second square of paper and crush it into the same shape as the hidden paper. Then show the paper in your open hand. Casually put your hands into your pockets, shoving the pocket linings back in and pushing the wadded paper up into the dead space of one pocket. Bring out your hand in a fist as though you are holding the paper. Then turn your back to the audience.

Watch where I throw this paper so that it can be picked up and put into the proper place.

Throw your hand up into the air, turn around, and watch the invisible paper fly.

Did anyone see where it landed? No? Maybe it's still in my pocket.

Turn your pocket inside out. The paper will remain hidden in the "dead" space.

I know exactly where it is. I'll always know where there is unwanted trash and probably who put it there. See, there it is!

Give the location.

Will someone pick it up, please, and put it in the recycling bin? Let's give him a round of thanks and applause!

Books to Share

Hadingham, Evan, and Janet Hadingham. *Garbage! Where It Comes From, Where It Goes.* Simon, 1990. Who creates garbage and solutions for disposal.

Wilcox, Charlotte. *Trash!* Art by Jerry Bushey. Carolrhoda, 1988. A survey of the subject of . . . trash.

The School Bus

THE EFFECT

The magician shows a picture. She cuts the picture in half, showing the two halves. Putting the two pieces together back to back, she cuts again, then opens the picture showing that it is still intact. The picture can be cut until it is reduced to the size needed to match the trick.

YOU WILL NEED

picture of a school bus   baby powder

rubber cement   scissors

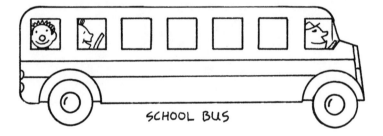

SCHOOL BUS

PREPARATION

Prepare the picture by duplicating and enlarging the school bus from this book and cutting it out. Then paint the back of the picture with a layer of rubber cement. Let it dry. Paint a second coat over the first. Let it dry. Dust the rubber cement with baby powder. This will keep the two pieces of paper from

The School Bus

1. CUT AND FOLD OVER THE REAR OF BUS

2. CUT END OFF FOLDED BUS

3. PUT BUS ENDS TOGETHER

4. CUT AND FOLD AGAIN

5. CUT END OFF FOLDED BUS

6. UNFOLD AND PUT ENDS TOGETHER

7. CUT AGAIN

8. FOLD AND TRIM END

UNFOLD MINIBUS

sticking to each other when they are placed back to back. The prepared picture can be stored for several months.

When performing the trick, you will want to first show the picture to your audience. Then cut it in half and show both halves to the audience. Put the two rubber cement sides together. Cut the end off the picture. Open the picture. The two ends will magically stick together, as long as you cut where the rubber cement has been painted.

PATTER AND PERFORMANCE

My father drives a school bus during the week. On weekends he is allowed to drive it just for fun. My Mom and I sit in the back of the bus while my Dad drives. Mom reads aloud to us as we admire the scenery. Dad complains that he can't hear my Mom read if she sits in the back of the bus.

"I'll make the bus smaller," she says. She cuts the bus in half.

Cut the bus in half. Show the audience one half with Dad driving, and one half with Mom and the daughter in the back of the bus. Place the two halves back to back and cut off the end, then open and display the smaller bus. (See illustrations 1–3.)

"I still can't hear you," shouts Dad. Mom cuts the bus again.

Cut the bus in half again, and repeat the process. (See illustrations 4–6.)

"No, still not small enough," shouts Dad.

Continue cutting the end off the bus and showing it opened until it is much smaller. (See illustrations 7–8.)

"Now I can hear you read," says Dad with a satisfied smile.

Show the new, smaller bus and take your bow.

Books to Share

Cole, Joanna. *The Magic School Bus Inside a Hurricane.* Art by Bruce Degen. Scholastic, 1995. Ms. Frizzle and her adventuresome class visit a hurricane.

Crews, Donald. *School Bus.* Art by author. Greenwillow, 1984. Ride the school bus.

Kovalski, Maryann. *The Wheels on the Bus.* Art by author. Little, 1987.

Raffi. *Wheels on the Bus.* Art by Sylvie Kantrovitz Wickstrom. Crown, 1988. Sing the song while sharing the pictures.

The Fish That Got Away

The same effect as that of the school bus getting smaller but remaining in one piece can be used with a picture of a fish.

PATTER AND PRESENTATION
Tell a story about your Dad claiming to catch the biggest fish in the world. Say that when you questioned him in disbelief, he changed his story (cutting the fish to make it smaller) until it was a small fish.

> Now I believe you, Dad. But if you had taken me with you, we would have more to eat for dinner. Of course, I catch really big fish!

Or read the following poem and show the fisherman from whom the fish escaped!

Fish Story
Richard Armour

Count this among my heartfelt wishes:
To hear a fish tale told by fishes
And stand among the fish who doubt
The honor of a fellow trout,
And watch the bulging of their eyes
To hear of imitation flies
And worms with rather droopy looks
Stuck through with hateful horrid hooks,
And fishermen they fled all day from
(as big as this) and got away from.

Books to Share

Share books featuring fish. See Books to Share on page 57.

Sawing a Rabbit in Half

Place a picture of a rabbit into a magician's "trunk." Cut the trunk in half and . . . presto! The rabbit appears unharmed.

YOU WILL NEED
envelope, any size, to serve as the magician's "trunk"

picture of a rabbit   scissors

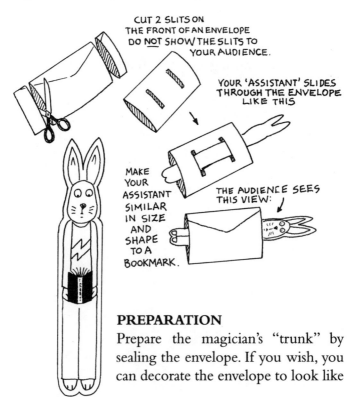

CUT 2 SLITS ON THE FRONT OF AN ENVELOPE DO **NOT** SHOW THE SLITS TO YOUR AUDIENCE.

YOUR 'ASSISTANT' SLIDES THROUGH THE ENVELOPE LIKE THIS

MAKE YOUR ASSISTANT SIMILAR IN SIZE AND SHAPE TO A BOOKMARK.

THE AUDIENCE SEES THIS VIEW:

PREPARATION
Prepare the magician's "trunk" by sealing the envelope. If you wish, you can decorate the envelope to look like

a trunk. Cut off both ends of the envelope. Make two slits in the front of the envelope.

Place the rabbit through the slits in the front of the envelope. The audience will see the head and feet of the rabbit, making it appear that the rabbit is in the "trunk."

PATTER AND PRESENTATION

A well-known trick often performed by stage magicians is to saw a woman in half. In this trick I will use my grandmother's trunk. It used to contain treasures from my grandparents' travels to Asia, but now, alas, it is empty.

Squeeze the envelope to make a tube and put your fingers into it to show that it is empty.

My assistant is my Reading Rabbit. I place him into the trunk.

Pretend to place the rabbit into the envelope as you actually place him through the slits in the front.

My saw is currently in the shop being sharpened, so I will use these scissors instead to cut the trunk in half.

CUT ONLY THE ENVELOPE....

... THE ASSISTANT ISN'T CUT!

Cut the envelope in half by placing the scissors in front of the rabbit but in back of the envelope. The audience will see that the envelope is cut in two pieces, but the rabbit remains in one piece.

Where are you, Rabbit? Safe and sound and still . . . reading! Let's give Rabbit a round of applause.

Show the two halves of the trunk, then remove the rabbit and let him take a bow.

Books to Share
Every spring there are new books featuring rabbits. Start with the following books, then explore your own library shelves.

Bernhard, Emery, and Durga Bernhard. *How Snowshoe Hare Rescued the Sun: A Tale from the Arctic.* Art by Durga Bernhard. Holiday, 1993. Hare brings the stolen sun back to the animals.

Han, Suzanne Crowder. *The Rabbit's Judgement.* Art by Yumi Heo. Holt, 1994. Told in both Korean and English, the rabbit arbitrates a dispute between the man and the tiger.

Johnston, Tony. *The Tale of Rabbit and Coyote.* Art by Tomie dePaola. Putnam, 1994. Rabbit outwits coyote in a Zapotec tale relating why coyote howls at the moon.

Hint

If you prefer, you can use a dollar bill instead of a rabbit and exhibit books about money.

Two Magic Tricks with Color

Red!

This trick can be adapted to use with any color program. It's truly magical!

THE EFFECT
A framed black-and-white picture is shown to the audience. It magically becomes full-color art.

YOU WILL NEED
a poster board frame with an acetate (clear plastic) window (Frames are available from art or stationery stores.)

access to a duplicating machine that will make transparencies (Or you can use a black permanent-marker pen directly on the acetate.)

a black-and-white line drawing and exactly the same drawing in color

a piece of white poster board cut to the same dimensions as the art

PREPARATION
Draw the illustration on a sheet of paper and copy it onto acetate (transparency film). In this case, draw Sam's picture of his room as described in the following story. Remember, you don't have to have training in fine art, for Sam is just a little boy. If you prefer,

however, you can simply duplicate the drawing shown here.

Make a duplicate of the line drawing, and color it liberally. If you plan to tell "Sam's Story," make your drawing predominantly red.

Next, sandwich the white poster board between the color picture and the acetate, and place all three pieces in the frame. The colored drawing will be on the bottom, then the blank poster board, then the clear acetate with the black-and-white drawing, and the frame on top. Now tape the color drawing and the black-and-white drawing together at the top with a small piece of clear tape. To "change" the black and white drawing to full color, simply pull the tape so that the color illustration and the black and white illustration emerge from the frame. Take it out slowly with the art facing your listeners so that they can see the picture magically changing to color in front of them. The black and white drawing will now be the outline for the colored drawing, so make sure that the two pictures are perfectly aligned when you tape them together.

PATTER AND PRESENTATION
Begin by reading "Sam's Story" to your group.

Sam's Story
Barbara Ann Porte

The day Sam stayed home from school with a cold, he finger painted. He showed me his pic-

POSTER BOARD

TAPE A WHITE POSTER BOARD
ALONG THE BOTTOM EDGE
OF A FRAME OF
THE SAME SIZE.

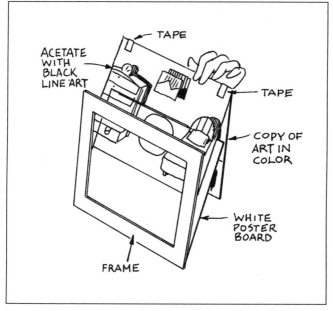

TAPE

ACETATE
WITH
BLACK
LINE ART

TAPE

COPY OF
ART IN
COLOR

WHITE
POSTER
BOARD

FRAME

ture. All of it was red. The paper was red, the table was red, the chairs all were red, and so were the lamp, the bowl on the table, and all the place settings. A bright red frog was perched on the arm of one chair.

"Why is everything red?" I asked. Sam was glad to explain.

"It's red *now*, but it didn't used to be. It used to be tan," he told me. "And I don't mean just this one room only. I mean the whole house and everything in it was tan. The walls were tan, the ceilings were tan, the floors were tan, the curtains were tan, and so was all of the furniture. Even the outside of the house was painted tan. The woman whose house it was liked tan. Well, she used to like tan. Even she was starting to get tired of it.

"One day the woman was on her way home from shopping. She had on her tan coat and tan hat. She was carrying a tan paper bag with groceries in it. Another woman was walking along, almost beside her. She was dressed all in red and was carrying a very large, red wicker basket.

"'What a pretty color that is,' the woman in tan said as the woman in red began to pass her.

"'Thank you,' said the woman holding the basket. 'I just bought it. It was too large to wrap, but I don't mind carrying it home this way. Just looking at it makes me feel cheerful.'

"Well, just looking at it made the woman in tan feel cheerful, too. I wouldn't mind carrying it, either, if it were mine, she said to herself as she reached her front door. She went inside and looked all around. 'Tan, tan, tan! It's enough already,' she told herself out loud.

"Very early the next morning, she got up, got dressed, ate breakfast, and went outside. She took the first bus going downtown." Sam stopped talking to catch his breath.

"I know what she did next," I said. "She went shopping and bought everything new in red. 'Please send it,' she told the salesperson. 'There's too much to carry.'"

"Oh, no, she didn't," said Sam. I could tell by his tone he didn't like my ending. "All that woman bought downtown was paint. Red paint. Then she took the bus home, changed her clothes, and went to work. She painted everything, inside and out. She painted her roof and her walls, her curtains and her floors, her table and chairs, her dishes and bowls, and even her silverware."

"You left out the frog. Did she paint the frog red, too?" I asked.

"Don't be silly, Abigail. You can't paint a frog. A frog is a living thing," Sam told me. "Besides, she didn't have to. It was a rare tomato frog from Madagascar, the same as at the zoo. It was red to start with, and anyway, it didn't move in until *after* the woman painted." Sam sneezed. Then he sneezed again.

"How's your cold?" Mom asked, sticking her head into the room just then.

"Fine. I feel much better," Sam said. He sneezed some more. Mom came closer and noticed his painting.

"Nice. It reminds me, though—I'm out of red. I meant to pick up some the other day at the store," she said.

"Maybe you can borrow some of Sam's," I said. Sam shook his head.

"I used up all of mine on this painting," he told us. Mom laughed.

"I'm not surprised. Next time I'm out, I'll pick up some for both of us," she told him.

"I'm out of red, too," I said.

"I'll buy enough for everyone. 'Red, red, red, nothing but red,' I'll tell the salesperson. 'You can never have too much of such a happy color.'" Then Mom touched Sam on his forehead. "You feel fine to me. I think you can go to school tomorrow," she said, and left the room, humming.

————————

I just happen to have one of the pictures that Sam drew the day he stayed home from school.

Show the black and white picture to the group. Describe the picture while the group is looking at it.

As you already know, this is just a sketch of the picture that Sam drew, because he used red paint for the final version. It looks like this.

Pull the line drawing and the color picture out of the frame, revealing Sam's red room.

Books to Share

Picó, Fernando. *The Red Comb.* Art by María Antonia Ordónez. Bridgewater, 1991. A little girl leaves her precious red comb for a runaway slave.

Stinson, Kathy. *Red Is Best.* Annick, 1982. A little girl loves the color red.

Wyllie, Stephen. *The Red Dragon.* Art by Jonathan Allen. Dial, 1993. Red Dragon changes his diet and becomes green.

Young, Ed. *Red Thread.* Art by author. Putnam, 1993. A man and woman will marry if their feet are tied with red thread.

The same effect can be used for any picture. Read my poem "Alone" using a black-and-white picture of animals that changes to a colored one reflecting the colors in the poem. Or read it followed by the next trick: the crayon color trick.

Alone, sort of

Caroline Feller Bauer

It could have been boring at home alone.
But I wasn't alone.
A red giraffe
standing next to a blue hippo
surrounded by green palm trees
kept me company.
You can have a lot of friends
if your Mom gives you
a new box of crayons.

Do you speak German? If so, you may prefer to read this version.

Alleine
translated by Chris Wendel

Zuhause hätte es alleine langweilig werden können.
Aber ich war nicht alleine.
Zu mir gesellte sich
eine rote Giraffe,
neben ihr ein blaues Nilpferd,
umgeben von grünen Palmen
Man kann eben viele Freunde haben,
wenn die Mutter einem
eine neue Schachtel bunter Farbstifte schenkt.

Crayon Color

THE EFFECT
A volunteer chooses a crayon from a box of crayons. The magician reveals the color the volunteer has chosen.

YOU WILL NEED
box of crayons
volunteer

PATTER AND PRESENTATION
A new box of crayons is always a treat. After you've colored many pictures, the crayons

become true friends. This particular box of crayons tells me what color to use when I'm drawing. I don't even need to see the crayon to tell which color has been taken from the box.

Michael (name of your volunteer), would you open the box of crayons and show it to the audience? I will turn around so that I cannot see the crayon you have chosen. (Turn around.)

Please take a crayon from the box and show it to the audience. Now, please give me the crayon.

Stretch your left hand out to receive the crayon and turn around to face the audience still holding the crayon, scraping a nail of your right hand over the crayon to dig out a bit of color.

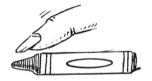

Let's see what color you've chosen. I think the crayon is talking to me.

Bring your right hand close to your face till you see the color chosen.

Yes. I think the crayon wants me to draw a flower in . . . (name color, then bring the crayon out from behind your back). Yes! Let's give a round of applause to Michael and another for the talking crayon.

Books to Share

"The Art of Art" in Bauer, Caroline Feller. *Celebrations.* Art by Lynn Bredeson. H.W. Wilson, 1985. A complete program with stories and poetry featuring color.

"De colores" in Orozco, Jose Luis, ed. *De Colores and Other Latin-American Folk Songs for Children.* Art by Elisa Kleven. Dutton, 1994. This happy song from Latin America is sung holding hands and swaying in time to the music.

Dewey, Ariane. *Naming Colors.* Art by author. Harper, 1995. Short explanations of how colors got their names in English.

Heifetz, Jeanne. *When Blue Meant Yellow: How Colors Got Their Names.* Holt, 1994. Short vignettes tracing the origins of color names.

Hoban, Tana. *Colors Everywhere.* Photos by author. Greenwillow, 1995. Glorious color photographs.

Oram, Hiawyn. *Out of the Blue: Poems about Color.* Art by David McKee. Hyperion, 1993. A collection of original poems about color.

Snack Pack

THE EFFECT

The magician shows an empty paper lunch sack, a pitcher of water, and an empty paper cup. Looking confused, she puts the cup in the paper bag, removes the empty cup from the bag, and pours water into the bag. Then she puts the cup back into the bag, removes the cup filled with water, shows the empty bag, and tosses it in the wastebasket.

YOU WILL NEED

2 paper cups

pitcher of water

paper sack

scissors

book

PREPARATION

Prepare one paper cup by cutting the bottom out. Prepare the other paper cup by cutting the rim from the top so that the bottomless cup nests in the rimless cup.

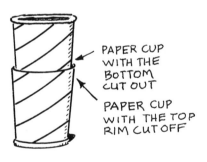

PAPER CUP WITH THE BOTTOM CUT OUT

PAPER CUP WITH THE TOP RIM CUT OFF

PATTER AND PRESENTATION

When I'm reading a book, I often like to drink something from time to time. Water is the right price, and it's healthy, too. I use a recycled paper cup.

Pick up the cup and show it to your audience.

My lunch was in this bag.

Show the empty sack to your audience.

And here is the water, fresh from the refrigerator.

Pick up the pitcher of water.

Let's see, I was in the middle of the last chapter of (name the title of your book and show it to the audience), but I'm thirsty so I'll just put the cup in the paper bag.

Place the cup in the bag.

Oh no, that's not what you do.

Take the cup out of the bag and place it on the table, looking puzzled. In doing so, you will actually remove the bottomless cup.

I pour the water into the bag.

Carefully pour a little water into the cup in the paper bag.

Oh no, that's not what you do. You must have a cup first.

Put the bottomless cup back in the paper bag into the now-filled rimless cup.

That's better!

Remove the cup of water and take a drink, then crush the cup in your hand, removing evidence of the trick! Pick up the paper bag and casually show that it is empty.

> I get so involved in my reading that I can't even take a drink of water properly! Luckily I remember how to read.

Sit down and start reading the paper bag.

Books to Share

Baer, Edith. *This Is the Way We Eat Our Lunch: A Book About Children Around the World*. Art by Steve Björkman. Scholastic, 1995. In a rhyming text, children from around the world enjoy their lunch.

Fleming, Denise. *Lunch*. Art by author. Holt, 1992. A mouse eats his way through a variety of collage cut-out fruits and vegetables.

Moore, Floyd C. *I Gave Thomas Edison My Sandwich*. Art by Donna Kae Nelson. Whitman, 1995. Floyd remembers the day he met Thomas Edison.

Pelham, David. *Sam's Sandwich*. Art by author. Dutton, 1990. Sam puts bugs and other surprises into Samantha's sandwich.

Fingers and Hands

These finger manipulations are among the first tricks that I remember. I was in nursery school when a magician showed us how he could detach his thumb from his hand. It was fascinating and a bit alarming. Try just one of these at a time along with a finger play or poem.

Remove Your Thumb

THE EFFECT
With one hand on top of the other, pull your thumb so that it appears as if it is being pulled off.

YOU WILL NEED
your 2 hands

PREPARATION
Practice making a fist with one hand, leaving the thumb pointed up. Then grasp the thumb in the fist of your other hand, putting the thumb between the first and second fingers. Grimace while you pull the top fist away from the first. Make it look as though your thumb is being stretched several inches. Then pull your top fist away from your bottom fist and tuck the thumb into the fist making it appear that the thumb has been detached.

Another version is this one: Make a fist, and tuck the top half of the left thumb into your fist so that the bottom half looks amputated. Hold right index finger over the knuckle of the right thumb, and bring right index finger and thumb to the top of the "amputated" left knuckle. Moving the right hand an inch away from the knuckle and then back will show how the thumb has been severed.

Even the youngest child will be aware that these are tricks, but children love them anyway, excitedly looking for the thumb—or half thumb—in your hand!

PATTER AND PRESENTATION

When I was a child I learned that one thing that separates humans from animals is that we have a thumb, enabling us to manipulate objects easily. Since then, I've always made sure to take my thumb with me wherever I go. In fact, sometimes I even take my thumb off, just to be certain that I don't lose it!

Count Your Fingers

THE EFFECT

The magician counts her fingers and finds that she has 11 instead of 10.

PATTER AND PRESENTATION

Hold up one hand and point to each finger as you count

One, two, three, four, five.

Now continue counting the fingers on your other hand.

Six, seven, eight, nine, ten. No, that's not possible. I know that I have 11.

Now count backward touching each finger.

Ten, nine, eight, seven, six, and (hold up the other hand) five makes eleven!

Finger Plays to Share

Right Hand, Left Hand

This is my right hand;
I'll raise it up high. *(Raise right hand.)*

This is my left hand;
I'll touch the sky. *(Raise left hand.)*

Right hand, left hand, *(Raise right hand,
raise left hand.)*

Roll them around. *(Roll hands around.)*

Right hand, left hand, *(Raise right hand,
raise left hand.)*

Pound, Pound, Pound. *(Pound fists together.)*

Open Them, Shut Them

(Follow actions of rhyme.)

Open them, shut them,
Give a little clap.
Open them, shut them,
Lay them in your lap.
Creep them, creep them,
Right up to your chin.
Open wide your mouth,
But do not let them in!

Open them, shut them,
Give a little clap.
Open them, shut them,
Lay them in your lap.
Creep them, creep them,
Right up to your cheek.
Put them over your eyes,
And through your fingers peek.

Where Is Thumbkin?

Where is thumbkin?   *(Start with hands behind back.)*
Where is thumbkin?

Here I am.   *(Bring fists forward and extend*
and Here I am.   *bend one thumb, then the other*
                with the rhyme.)

How are you today, sir?
How are you today, sir?

Very well, I thank you.
Very well, I thank you.

Run away.   *(Move hand behind back.)*
Run away.

The rhyme can be repeated with the other fingers:
pointer, tall one, ring finger, and pinky.

Quiet! We're Listening

(Follow actions as indicated.)

Sometimes my hands are at my side;
Then behind my back they hide.
Sometimes I wiggle fingers so,
Shake them fast, shake them slow.
Sometimes my hands go clap, clap, clap.
Then I rest them in my lap.
Now they're quiet as can be.
Because it's listening time for me.

The Magician's Hands

J. Patrick Lewis

Fly at light-speed . . .
He can make you believe
In make-believe—
That the Queen of Hearts
is a turtle dove,
That an egg can open
To a bouquet of flowers.

As the colored scarves
Rainbow endlessly
From his mouth,
You hang on the cliff
Edge of wonder.

Watch. Watch him
Very carefully.
Your imagination
Is the only thing he has
Up his sleeve.

The Magic Animals

THE EFFECT

A volunteer thinks of an animal; the magician identifies the chosen animal.

YOU WILL NEED

1 picture of each of the following six animals: lion, horse, monkey, chicken, elephant, butterfly

easel or blackboard to which you can attach the pictures

PREPARATION

Practice with a friend! He can play the part of the volunteer you will select from the audience. Ask him to choose an animal from those you have displayed (in random order) without telling you which animal he has chosen. Then ask him to silently spell the name of the animal as you point to each animal on the board, stopping when he reaches the last letter of his animal. When he stops, you will be pointing to the animal he has chosen!

You may begin by pointing to any three animals in any order, but the fourth one must be the lion, and you must continue in this order: horse, monkey, chicken, elephant, butterfly. Make sure you memorize the sequence, or write the list on your hand! When your volunteer reaches the last letter of his animal, you will be pointing to that animal.

PATTER AND PRESENTATION

Here are six animals. (Name each animal.) Amazingly, they have been trained to spell. Please think of one of the animals, but don't tell me which one you have chosen. I will point to each animal, and as I point, you think of the first letter of the animal you have chosen. As I point to the next animal, think of the next letter of the animal you have chosen, and so on, until you reach the last letter of your animal. Then say "stop!" Magically, I will be pointing to the animal you have chosen. Let's begin.

Hint

Make sure that your volunteer knows how to spell the names of the animals. If in doubt, label the pictures.

Books to Share

Facklam, Margery. *What Does the Crow Know? The Mysteries of Animal Intelligence.* Art by Pamela Johnson. Sierra Club, 1994. Explores the intelligence of domestic and wild animals.

Lacome, Julie. *Walking through the Jungle.* Art by author. Candlewick, 1993. A little boy walks through the jungle past a variety of wild animals.

Mayo, Margaret. *Tortoise's Flying Lesson: Animal Stories.* Art by Emily Bolam. Harcourt, 1995. Eight short stories with lively illustrations.

McDonnell, Flora. *I Love Animals.* Art by author. Candlewick, 1994. A little girl names all the animals on the farm.

Tomb, Howard, and Dennis Kunkel. *MicroAliens: Dazzling Journeys with an Electron Microscope.* Farrar, 1993. Amazing close-ups of the smallest animals, from dust mites to cat fleas.

Treasure Beads

Use this effect whenever you tell a story in which a mean-spirited person is tricked by a fool, or when treasure is the prize won in a story. Included here is a wonderful Czech story in which a poor woman and her rooster become rich with jewels.

THE EFFECT
The audience is shown a jar of colored beads. When the beads are transferred to a bag, a member of the audience chooses a bead from the bag. The magician identifies the color of the bead chosen.

YOU WILL NEED
20 colored beads in a variety of colors (available from a craft or bead shop)

20 beads of the same color

transparent jar or glass that will hold all the beads

cloth bag (large enough to hold the beads and roomy enough to accommodate the hand of the volunteer)

transparent thread (on which to string the beads)

small table

volunteer

PREPARATION
String the various colored beads onto the transparent thread and tie into a circle. Put the string of beads

and the loose beads into a jar. Put the jar and the cloth bag on the table.

PATTER AND PRESENTATION

This is my collection of jewels. I have diamonds, rubies, sapphires, and pearls.

Briefly show the jar of beads.

And this is my jewel bag.

Show the bag, turning it inside out to show that it is empty.

I'm going to put my jew-els into this bag so that I can carry it with me.

Dump the beads into the bag. Put your hand in the bag and gather the string of beads well into your palm. Keep your hand in the bag, holding the inside edge of the bag with it.

LOOSE BEADS
ARE ALL THE SAME
COLOR

I'm going to ask (give the name of your volunteer) to help me. "David," would you please put your hand in the bag and take a jewel—only one, please—but don't let me see it.

Hold the bag slightly higher than the volunteer's eye level so that he can't see into the bag.

Do you have a jewel? Good. Now, ladies and gentleman, David could have taken a ruby, an emerald, or an amethyst, but he took a blue sap-phire. Isn't that correct?

David will reply "yes," since the loose beads are all the same color. Ask him to show the bead to the audience.

Of course, another way to obtain a jewel is to make friends with the rooster who tricked a king!

The Rooster and the Diamond

A long, long time ago when your great great grandfather was young there lived an old woman. She lived in a hut on a small piece of ground. She had no cow. She had no donkey, but she owned a fine rooster. He hunted for food in the dusty road that wound past the old woman's house. The woman would sit on a stool outside the hut and watch the rooster as he pecked in the dirt searching for insects.

One bright day the rooster was busily peck, peck, pecking in the road. Instead of finding some tasty insects, the rooster saw a shiny object and picked it up in his beak. It was a large diamond. The rooster was going to bring it to the old woman when along came the king.

The king was a roly poly man. In fact, he was quite fat. He was probably one of the biggest men in the country, not tall mind you, but broad. He enjoyed a good hearty meal. He was so rotund that he had to have servants to help him walk. On this fine day, he wasn't walking, he was riding in a carriage. He spotted the spirited rooster holding a large diamond in his mouth. "Ho!," he shouted. "Bring that rooster to me."

One of the servants obliged and scooped up the rooster from the road and carried him back to the king. "Look! The rooster is holding a diamond in his beak. I'll have that," the king said as he grabbed the diamond from the rooster's beak. The rooster was dropped back onto the road.

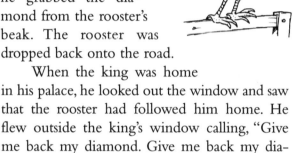

When the king was home in his palace, he looked out the window and saw that the rooster had followed him home. He flew outside the king's window calling, "Give me back my diamond. Give me back my diamond."

"The rooster has followed us to the palace," said the king. "Take the rooster out to the well and drown him."

The servants took the rooster to the well and left him there. The rooster called out, "Come my empty stomach, drink up all the water." All the water from the well flew into the rooster's stomach.

The rooster flew to the king's palace window, and flapping his wings he called, "Give me back my diamond. Give me back my diamond."

"Ho," said the king. "The rooster is back. Take him to the courtyard where the fire is burning. Throw him in the fire."

The servants took the rooster to the fire

and left him there. The rooster called out, flapping his wings. "Come my full stomach, empty out all the water." The water from the well came out of the rooster and put out the fire.

The rooster flew to the king's palace window, and flapping his wings he called, "Give me back my diamond. Give me back my diamond."

"Ho," said the king, "that rooster is back. Take him to the garden where the royal beehives are placed. Let the bees sting him."

The servants took the rooster to the royal beehives and left him there. The rooster flapped his wings calling, "Come my empty stomach, drink up all the bees." The bees flew into the rooster's stomach.

The rooster flew to the king's palace window, and flapping his wings he called, "Give me back my diamond. Give me back my diamond."

"Ho," said the king, "that rooster is back. Bring him here into the throne room. I'll sit on him, and he will be finished."

The servants brought the rooster into the throne room. The servants set the rooster on a red silk cushion. The enormously fat king slowly began to ease himself on top of the rooster.

The rooster flapped his wings and called, "Come my full stomach. Come my full stomach, empty out all the bees." The bees flew out of the rooster's stomach and of course they stung the king. Even though he didn't often move very fast, it looked as though the king was dancing a lively jig.

"Ho," shouted the king, "give the rooster back his diamond."

The diamond had already been taken to the king's treasure room. The servants took the rooster to the treasure room so that he could find the diamond. Baskets and boxes were piled high with jewels. There were diamonds and rubies, pearls and emeralds. Gold and silver coins glistened in the lights of torches.

The rooster flapped his wings and called, "Come my empty stomach. Come my empty stomach. Drink up all the jewels." The jewels and coins flew into the rooster's stomach.

When the rooster flew home to the poor woman's house he landed at the woman's feet. Flapping his wings he called, "Come my full stomach. Come my full stomach. Empty out all the jewels." All the jewels from the treasure house flew out onto the floor of the hut.

The woman was rich. The rooster slept on a pink satin cushion and ate golden corn from a silver dish.

And the king? He is still taking lots of hot baths to soothe his ego and his bee bites.

Stories and Books to Share

The hero of "The Rooster and the Diamond" is a rooster. Share other books and stories—both new and old—about chickens, roosters, and ducks.

STORIES TO TELL

"The Prince Who Was a Rooster," in Bauer, Caroline Feller. *New Handbook for Storytellers.* ALA, 1993.

A prince, tired of his studies, pretends to be a rooster. Act this one out.

"The Young Rooster," in Lobel, Arnold. *Fables.* Art by author. Harper, 1980. A rooster wakes the sun for the first time.

BOOKS TO READ

Joyce, William. *Bently & Egg.* Art by author. Harper, 1992. Bently, the frog, is put in charge of a duck's egg.

Lewison, Wendy Cheyette. *The Rooster Who Lost His Crow.* Art by Thor Wickstrom. Dial, 1995. Rooster loses his crow and searches all over the farm until he finds it.

McCloskey, Robert. *Make Way for Ducklings.* Art by author. Viking, 1941. The famous book about ducks in Boston.

Porte, Barbara Ann. *Chickens! Chickens!* Art by Greg Henry. Orchard, 1995. "There once was a man who drew chickens—chickens, chickens, nothing but chickens."

Scamell, Ragnhild. *Rooster Crows.* Art by Judith Riches. Tambourine, 1994. Rooster bets that he can crow the sun up at midnight.

Silverman, Erica. *Don't Fidget a Feather!* Art by S. D. Schindler. Macmillan, 1994. Duck swims faster and Gander flies higher, but who will be the champion of standing without fidgeting a feather?

On the Range

This is a popular effect with many versions. I've used this particular version of the "cut-and-restored" rope trick lots of times. One of my favorite treatments is to use a patter that introduces an audience to me as an author. The rope represents the book that I'm writing. When I cut the rope, I am cutting out a paragraph that I don't like. But I restore the rope if my editor says that the portion I removed was her favorite part!

Here's another theme that is ideal with the rope trick. Recently, there have been a variety of books published featuring cowhands and ranch life. And since ropes are used on a ranch, you have a perfect topic to use with your trick. A rope trick is also fun to use with patter about ships and the sea. Here is the trick and the patter that I use with my ranch theme.

THE EFFECT
The magician shows a length of rope. She cuts it in half, then restores it to its original length.

YOU WILL NEED
length of rope at least 3 feet long
scissors

PREPARATION
You will definitely want to practice this several times before you perform in public, but the secret is easily mastered.

1. Take end *A* of the rope between the thumb and fore-finger of your left hand, letting the rope hang down so that end *B* is pointing to the floor.

2. Take end *B* in your right hand and bring it up to end *A*, grasping both ends between your left thumb and left forefinger

3. You now have a loop hanging down in the middle.

4. With your right hand, bring the loop up to your left hand. Lay the loop on top of end *B* and grasp it firm-ly. You are now holding ends *A* and *B* and the loop in your left hand between the thumb and forefinger. (Don't panic! If I can do this trick, so can you.)

5. Bring part of end *B* from under the loop and make another loop.

6. Pull up the loop you just made. The audience will believe that what they are seeing is the middle of the rope, but in truth it is only this small loop.

7. Cut this small loop with the scissors.

8. Drop end *A* and end *B* from your hand. It will appear as though you are holding the two ends of the rope. In reality, however, you are holding a two- or three-inch piece of rope on either side of the original rope.

9. With the ends of this short piece of rope, tie a knot girdling the longer rope, tight enough to grip it but not too tight to slide.

10. Release your fist. You will now have a length of rope with a knot tied "in" it that you will show to your audience.

11. Cover the knot with your right hand.

12. Pass the rope through your left hand, coiling it as you go. You are pulling the knot off the rope as it passes through your left hand with your right hand.

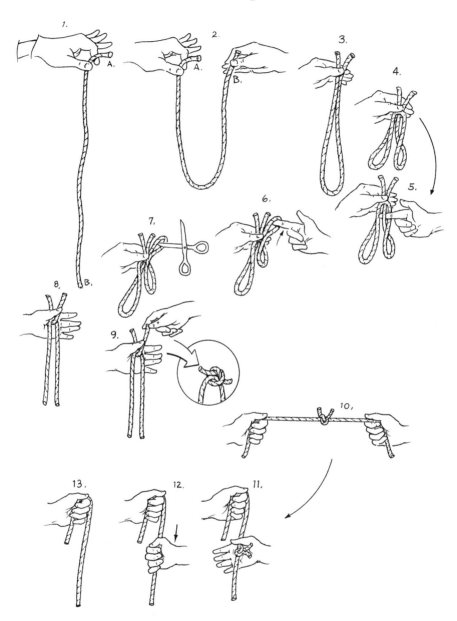

13. When you show the restored rope, you can take your bow.

Your audience is so impressed that they will not see you hide the knot in your pocket. You don't even need to feel anxious about getting rid of the knot immediately. Hold it in your palm as you change the subject and begin showing the books you want to share.

PATTER AND PRESENTATION

My Grandpa moved out west in '88. He was always talking about the good old days in the big city, but my Grandma loved her new life on the ranch. She was a real champion with a lasso.

Twirl the rope.

One day she was all alone on the range—well, not exactly alone, for she was driving 2,000 head of cattle—when out from behind a boulder jumped Badland Karl. Most people would run as fast as an antelope to get far away from the famous cattle rustler, but not my Grandma Paula.

"Out for a stroll in the desert I see," said Paula, twirling her rope. "Guess I may have to tie you up and leave you here without even a book to read. See this here rope? It's got two ends and a middle too. I'm going to cut out the middle just to show you what you'll look like if you don't just skedaddle right out of here.

Extend the rope to show its entire length. Without saying it, you are demonstrating that you are using one unbroken piece of rope. Follow directions as you tell the story.

"Or maybe I'll just tie you up. On the other hand, maybe that's not such a good idea. I guess I'll just put this rope back together. I don't think you'll want to mess about with a magical cowgirl."

Try to time your actions so that the story ends with the restoration of the rope.

My grandma ignored the frightened look on Badland Karl's face and continued driving her cattle to market and twirling her rope.

Books to Share

Anderson, Joan. *Cowboys: Roundup on an American Ranch.* Photographs by George Ancona. Scholastic, 1996. A photo essay of a roundup.

Garland, Sarah. *Tex the Cowboy.* Art by author. Dutton, 1995. Follow Tex through his comic book adventures.

Johnston, Tony. *The Cowboy and the Blackeyed Pea.* Art by Warren Ludwig. Putnam, 1992. In this take-off of Hans Christian Andersen's "The Princess and the Pea," a cowboy wins a princess by feeling a pea under a pile of saddle blankets.

Martin, Bill, Jr. *White Dynamite and Curly Kidd.* Art by Ted Rand. Holt, 1986. Is that a girl on that horse?

Scott, Ann Herbert. *A Brand Is Forever.* Art by Ronald Himler. Clarion, 1993. A little girl learns to brand a calf with her own brand. The book has more text than most picture books. (Also see *Cowboy Country* by the same author.)

Shepard, Aaron. *The Legend of Lightning Larry.* Art by Toni Goffe. Scribner's, 1993. Larry Lightning shoots from the heart and the outlaws turn into nice guys.

Toriseva, JoNelle. *Rodeo Day.* Art by Robert Casilla. Bradbury, 1994. Lacey competes in her first rodeo.

A Book for a Desert Island

THE EFFECT

A story is told using a paper boat. After tearing off the bow, stern, and mast, a T-shirt with the word *read* on it is revealed.

YOU WILL NEED

2 sheets of newspaper or wrapping paper approximately 20″ × 30″

felt tip pen

Hint

> Any rectangular paper can be used, but since you are tearing a double thickness of paper, this will be harder to tear if it is heavier than newspaper.

PREPARATION

Print or write the word "*READ*" on one side of each paper. This will be the side that is on the inside of the boat before it is torn. Then make two boats (one sheet for each), following the directions. When each boat is folded, print *S.S. Read-a-Book* on the bow.

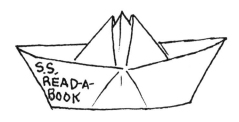

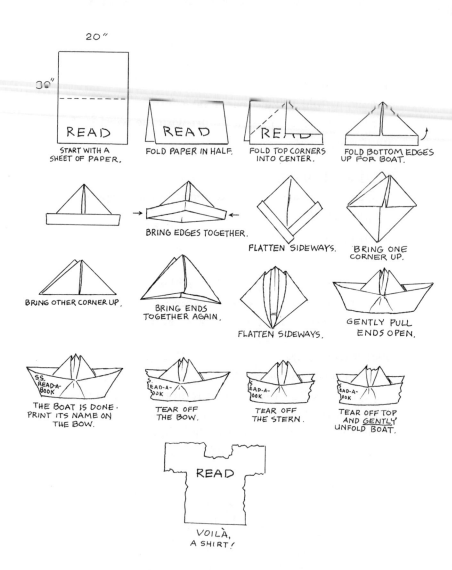

20″

30″

READ
START WITH A
SHEET OF PAPER.

READ
FOLD PAPER IN HALF.

READ
FOLD TOP CORNERS
INTO CENTER.

FOLD BOTTOM EDGES
UP FOR BOAT.

BRING EDGES TOGETHER.

FLATTEN SIDEWAYS.

BRING ONE
CORNER UP.

BRING OTHER CORNER UP.

BRING ENDS
TOGETHER AGAIN.

FLATTEN SIDEWAYS.

GENTLY PULL
ENDS OPEN.

SS,
READ-A-
BOOK
THE BOAT IS DONE.
PRINT ITS NAME ON
THE BOW.

EAD-A-
OOK
TEAR OFF
THE BOW.

EAD-A-
OOK
TEAR OFF
THE STERN.

EAD-A-
OOK
TEAR OFF TOP
AND GENTLY
UNFOLD BOAT.

READ
VOILÀ,
A SHIRT!

PATTER AND PERFORMANCE

One of the most frequent questions asked of book lovers is "What book would you take with you to a desert island?" This question has intrigued me and I find that I constantly change my mind about which book I would actually take with me. Would I take a practical book, such as a survival guide, or would I take a really fat novel that might last as long as it takes to be rescued from the island?

At this point you can stop your patter to share your current choices or you can show and exhibit the books after you finish the trick.

To test the validity of my choice of a book, I took a trip with my friend to a desert island. Who would like to be my traveling companion?

Choose someone from the audience, ask her name, and introduce her.

"Pam" is an experienced ship captain with her own boat, so we decided that we would each sail our own ship.

This effect is more fun when you have a volunteer or even two volunteers, each with her own boat. Quietly ask your volunteer to follow your actions.

Here are our twin ships: the *S.S. Read-a-Book* and the *S.S. Read-a-Book*. (Pronounce one in the present tense and one in the past tense.) Pam, here is your boat. We sailed from the port on a sunny day. The wind came up and we sailed forward and backward and around.

Move your boat as you speak. Your volunteer should follow your actions.

> On the second day there was a terrible storm. It grew so stormy that we couldn't see through the wind and the foam. The boats were thrown up and down and around. We both hit the same rock at the same time.

Tear off the bow and make sure that your volunteer is following your lead.

> The boat was still afloat as we sailed forward, backward, and around. Once again it hit a rock. This time the sterns were ripped from the boats.

Tear off the stern and make sure that your volunteer does the same.

> Yet the boats were still afloat, so we sailed forward, backward, and around. When we turned upside down our masts were destroyed.

Tear off the point of the boats.

> Now we were in the ocean, but we were able to swim to the shore of a desert island. Luckily our book bag was waterproof. We are still waiting to be rescued, but we spend our time sitting under a palm tree, wearing our T-shirts, and reading.

As you are speaking, open the remainder of the boat to reveal the T-shirt that says *READ*. Make sure that your volunteer does the same, then take your bows.

Books to Share

Burningham, John. *Mr. Gumpy's Outing.* Art by author. Holt, 1971. A boat finally capsizes after a group of animals overfills it.

Cecil, Laura, ed. *A Thousand Yards of Sea: A Collection of Sea Stories and Poems.* Art by Emma Chichester Clark. Greenwillow, 1992. Rudyard Kipling, Jack Prelutsky, Margaret Mahy, and others are represented in this collection.

Cousins, Lucy. *Noah's Ark.* Art by reteller. Candlewick, 1993. Sparse retelling with vivid art makes this a Noah to share.

Hawkins, Colin. *Pirate Ship.* Art by author. Cobblehill, 1994. A silly story with sprightly art accompanies a spectacular pop-up of a pirate ship.

Macauley, David. *Ship.* Art by author. Houghton, 1993. Archeologists search for a long-lost caravel in a fictionalized but information-filled story.

McDonnell, Flora. *I Love Boats.* Art by author. Candlewick, 1995. A little girl lists her favorite boats.

Platt, Richard. *Stephen Biesty's Cross-Sections Man-of-War.* Art by Stephen Biesty. Dorling Kindersley, 1993. Shows the life and times of a typical ship of the Napoleonic era.

BOOKS TO TAKE TO A DESERT ISLAND

Now that your young people have been charmed into books, what about you? Here are five of my favorite adult titles for a survival kit.

China Court by Rumer Godden. Because it will make you remember that books are treasure.

Crossing to Safety by Wallace Stegner. Because you need a friend.

French Lessons by Alice Kaplan. Because it reminds you that learning is wonderful.

Hotel Pastis by Peter Mayle. Because you need a place to stay.

A Suitable Boy by Vikram Seth. Because it's so long you'll have plenty of time to finish it before you are rescued.

Beyond the Beginning
Resources

Clubs

An excellent way to continue introducing magic and books to young people—and make friends at the same time—is to join a magic club. There may be a local branch of a national or international magicians' organization within driving distance of your town. If not, why not find an interested pen pal with whom you can correspond about magic? The following organizations have yearly conventions well worth attending and publish their own monthly journals.

International Brotherhood of Magicians
    P.O. Box 192090
    St. Louis, MO 63119
    (314) 638-6406   Fax (314) 638-6708

Society of American Magicians
    P.O. Box 510260
    St. Louis, MO 63151
    (314) 846-5659   Fax (314) 846-5659

Young Member Program of the
   Society of American Magicians
      Margaret Dailey
      7101 Buick Dr.
      Indianapolis, IN   46214-3224
      (317) 243-0774

Journals

The following journals publish articles about present
and past magicians, reviews of commercial tricks and
books, magic routines, and news of club conventions.

Genii
      The International Conjuror's Magazine
      929 S. Longwood Ave.
      Los Angeles, CA 90019
      (213) 935-2848

The Linking Ring
      International Brotherhood of Magicians
      P.O. Box 192090
      St. Louis, MO 63119
      (314) 638-6406   Fax (314) 638-6708

Magic
      Stan Allen and Associates
      7380 S. Eastern Ave., Ste. 124-179
      Las Vegas, NV 89123

The Magic Symbol
> The Young Member Program of the
> Society of American Magicians
> Margaret Dailey
> 7101 Buick Dr.
> Indianapolis, IN 46214-3224
> (317) 243-0774

M-U-M
> Society of American Magicians
> P.O. Box 510260
> St. Louis, MO 63151
> (314) 846-5659   Fax (314) 846-5659

Suppliers

The magic dealers in the following list will sell you their catalogs, or you can order from their ads in the journals. They also hold magic conventions. You can also contact the Magic Dealers' Association (4136 N. 37th St., Tacoma, WA 98407) for a magic dealer in your area.

Abbott's Magic Co.
> 124 St. Joseph St.
> Colon, MI 49040
> (616) 432-3235   Fax (616) 432-3357

David Ginn
> 4387 St. Michaels Dr.
> Lilburn, GA 30247
> (404) 923-1899

Hades Publications
P.O. Box 1414
Calgary, Alberta T2P 2L6 Canada
(403) 254-0160   Fax (403) 254-0456

Hank Lee's Magic Factory
P.O. Box 789
Medford, MA 02155
800-874-7400   Fax (617) 395-2034

Perfect Magic
4781 Van Horne Ave., Ste. 206
Montreal, Quebec H3W 1J1 Canada

Samuel Patrick Smith
P.O. Box 769
Tavares, FL 32778

Stevens Magic Emporium
3238 E. Douglas
Wichita, KS 67208
(316) 683-9582   Fax (316) 686-2442

Louis Tannen, Inc.
24 W. 25th St., 2d Floor
New York, NY 10010
(212) 929-4500   Fax (212) 929-4565

Steve Taylor
P.O. Box 301231
Portland, OR 97230

Videos

If you learn more easily by watching than by reading, you may want to order a video on magic.

Amazing Secrets of Card Magic: 15 Easy
   Card Tricks Anyone Can Do!
      Michael Ammar
      P.O. Box 100
      Tahoma, CA 96142

The Greater Magic Video Library
      Gene Anderson
      Stevens Magic Emporium
      3238 E. Douglas
      Wichita, KS 67208

The Magic of Books
      Bob Hargraves
      36 Kennedy Dr.
      Warwick, RI 02889

Magic of Reading
      B. J. Hickman
      625 Sixth St.
      Dover, NH 03820

Magic They Love to See
      David Ginn
      4387 St. Michaels Dr.
      Lilburn, GA 30247

Strong Magic with Silks
    Duane Laflin
    P.O. Box 228
    Sterling, CO 80751

CD-ROM

Learn the Art of Magic, featuring Jay Alexander, magician, teaches twenty-six magic tricks and includes material on the history of famous magicians.

Broderbund Software
    500 Redwood Blvd.
    Novato, CA 94948
    (415) 382-4400
    Fax (415) 382-4587

Internet

Like everything else, magic is spreading across the Internet and its World Wide Web. A good roundup of offerings (including a Houdini Web site) as of early 1996 appears in the magazine *M-U-M* (see under journals), vol. 85, no. 9, February 1996. Issue theme: "Magic Online." Among magazines with their own Web sites is *Magic: The Independent Magazine for Magicians* (http://www.magic-mag.com/), featuring teasers from articles, new tricks, listings, and news.

Books

Explore your local library and bookstore for magic titles. Keep in mind that many books are self-published by devoted magicians. These can be found through magic dealers and displayed at conventions.

Books Featuring Magic for Children

Baker, James W. *The Holiday Magic Books.* Art by George Overlie. Learner, 1988. The series includes *New Year's Magic, Valentine's Magic,* and *Birthday Magic.* Small books of theme magic with easy-to-perform effects.

Baillie, Marilyn, ed. *Magic Fun.* Little, 1992. Cards, paper, and mind magic in an oversize format for children.

Cobb, Vicki. *Magic . . . Naturally!* Art by Lionel Kalish. Harper, rev. ed. 1993. Science experiments as magic tricks.

Friedhoffer, Bob. *The Magic Show: A Guide for Young Magicians.* Art by Linda Eisenberg. Millbrook, 1994. Tricks are divided into easy, intermediate, and advanced.

Kettelkamp, Larry. *Magic Made Easy.* Art by Loring Eutemey. Morrow, rev. ed. 1981. Photographs and drawings further explain the secrets behind these tricks.

McGill, Ormond. *Mind Magic.* Art by Anne Canevari Green. Millbrook, 1995. Instructions for tricks that allow the magician to read minds.

Oxlade, Chris. *Science Magic with Magnets.* Barrons, 1995. Tricks with magnets.

Watts, Barry. *The Amazing Magic Book.* Art by Mark David. Harper, 1992. Twenty-two tricks for beginning magicians.

White, Laurence, Jr., and Ray Broekel. *Shazam! Simple Science Magic.* Art by Meyer Seltzer. Whitman, 1991. How to do it and the science behind the tricks.

Wyler, Rose, and Gerald Ames. *Magic Secrets.* Art by Arthur Dorros. Harper, rev. ed. 1990. An I Can Read Book of simple magic tricks. Also see *Spooky Tricks* by the same authors.

Books Featuring Magic for Adults

Adair, Ian. *100 Magic Tricks.* Book Sales (110 Enterprise Ave., Secaucus, NJ 07094), 1991. Large format with color photographs to help you prepare and perform.

Bird, Malcolm, and Alan Dart. *The Magic Handbook.* Chronicle, 1992. The cartoon drawings will help adults and children learn traditional magic tricks.

Blackstone, Harry. *Blackstone's Tricks Anyone Can Do.* Carol (120 Enterprise Ave., Secaucus, NJ 07094), 1993. Two hundred tricks from a well-known professional.

Ginn, David. *Clown Magic.* Art by Jim Kleefeld. Piccadilly (P.O. Box 25203, Colorado Springs, CO 80936), 1993. A professional children's magician tells the secrets of magic and clowning. Also see *Money Math Magic* by the same author. For a complete list and ordering information for books by David Ginn, write to him at 4387 St. Michaels Dr., Lilburn, GA 30247. He is a prolific author of books featuring "you can do it too" commercial tricks and traditional children's effects.

Hargraves, Bob. *A Lesson in Magic*. Art by Alan Wassilak. Hargraves (36 Kennedy Dr., Warwick, RI 02889), 1992. Hargraves was an elementary school teacher who uses his experience to describe routines for children.

Johnson, Anne Akers. *The Buck Book*. Klutz (2121 Staunton Ct., Palo Alto, CA 94306), 1993. If you can follow these directions you will be able to fold a dollar bill into a jumping frog, a bow tie, an elephant, and more.

Johnson, Marshall. *Consumer's Buying Guide to Magic* (1001 Flame Vine Ave. #204, Delray Beach, FL 33445-5904), 1995. A magician's recommendations for buying commercial tricks.

Ragsdale, Bill. *Magic Around the World*. Adventures in Entertainment (532 S. Hamilton St., Eden, NC 27288), 1994. The theme is flags from the world with accompanying effects. A video of the entire performance is also available.

Smith, Samuel Patrick. *Kiddie Patter and Little Feats*. SPS (P.O. Box 769, Tavares, FL 32778), 1993. "How to entertain pre-schoolers with magic and funny stuff." Excellent directions and patter for several complete routines using commercial tricks.

Tarr, Bill. *101 Easy-to-Do Magic Tricks.* Art by Frank Daniel. Dover, 1977. A little of everything: napkin tricks, paper tricks, water hat trick, and shadow effects.

Wilson, Mark. *Magic Tricks.* Running (125 S. 22nd St., Philadelphia, PA 19103), 1993. A stage performer shares both simple and advanced tricks.

Say the magic words
"THE END"
and watch this book
come to life!

$\mathcal{C}$aroline **Feller Bauer** is an author and presenter known throughout the world for her ideas on bringing children and books together. From Algeria to Zambia and in some sixty other nations including the U.S., she has delighted parents, children, librarians, and other educators with her creative reading-motivation techniques.

As a children's librarian in New York City, a school librarian in Colorado, and a library school professor in Oregon, Dr. Bauer's mission has been to find methods of introducing anyone to the joys of reading. One of those methods is magic. "If you have a magic trick in your pocket and a book to go with it, it's easy to make friends no matter where you are," she says. Dr. Bauer is a member of the Society of American Magicians, the International Brotherhood of Magicians, and a magician member of the Magic Castle in Los Angeles.

Recipient of many awards, she is the author of the classic *Caroline Feller Bauer's New Handbook for Storytellers* (ALA, cloth and paperback, 1993) and six other books. Dr. Bauer lives in Miami Beach, Florida, with her husband, Peter, who is always willing to see another magic trick or read a new book, and with a friendly ferret whose best trick is to disappear into any convenient box or bag.

Hugs,
Caroline Feller Bauer